THE HUNT FOR KIMATHI

IAN HENDERSON, G.M.

THE HUNT
FOR
KIMATHI

BY

IAN HENDERSON
G.M.

WITH

PHILIP GOODHART
M.P.

HAMISH HAMILTON

LONDON

First published in Great Britain, 1958
by Hamish Hamilton Ltd
90 Great Russell Street London WC1

PRINTED IN GREAT BRITAIN
BY WESTERN PRINTING SERVICES LTD BRISTOL

TO
MY WIFE MARIE
I.H.

CONTENTS

7

ILLUSTRATIONS

NOTE

In order to conceal the identities of pseudo-terrorists, no
recognizable photographs have been included.

FOREWORD

By

Richard Catling, c.m.g., o.b.e., Commissioner of Police, Kenya

IAN HENDERSON'S story is an account of the most important pseudo-gang operation of the whole campaign against Mau Mau terrorists in Kenya. The operation was designed to apprehend Dedan Kimathi, militant head of Mau Mau, and it succeeded.

The pseudo-gang technique was not evolved in Kenya; it was used many years earlier both in Palestine, during the Arab and Jewish rebellions in that country, and subsequently in Malaya against the Chinese Communist terrorists. But it achieved its widest measure of success in Kenya.

This book is confined to the single operation which resulted in Kimathi's capture. Yet the story epitomizes the tactics used by Field Intelligence Officers in the earlier days of the emergency, carried a step further by Special Force Teams led by Army, Administrative and Police Officers at a later stage, and ultimately perfected and executed with boldness, great courage and outstanding success by Henderson himself.

How was he able to convert captured Mau Mau terrorists to his own use almost overnight? If a brief answer to this is possible it is that his deep knowledge of the Kikuyu people, their language and their customs enabled him to reach into their minds and influence their thoughts in the way he wished. He knew the enemy as did few, if any, other Europeans in Kenya's Security Forces.

Nairobi, 30th December 1957

11

PART ONE

THE BACKGROUND

Chapter One

A REIGN OF TERROR

EARLY in the afternoon of the 7th of October 1952 Chief Waruhiu was shot and killed seven miles outside Nairobi. He was murdered in the best Chicago style. His car was forced to a halt by the side of the road, three gunmen then walked over to him and opened fire at point-blank range. The Chief's funeral was impressive. It was attended by several thousand of his fellow Kikuyu tribesmen. The new Governor, Sir Evelyn Baring, was there, and so was Jomo Kenyatta, then the most prominent African politician in Kenya. The size and eminence of the congregation was in part a tribute to Waruhiu's position and personality—he had been a chief for thirty years, and had received the M.B.E. earlier that year. In part it was also a recognition of the extraordinary circumstances surrounding Waruhiu's death. This was just one of many murders and acts of violence ascribed to Mau Mau, the secret, subversive movement that was growing increasingly bold. A few days before his death, Chief Waruhiu had condemned Mau Mau. The bullets in his head and stomach were the terrorists' reply.

For two more weeks the violence and rumours of violence spread. Then a state of emergency was proclaimed throughout the colony of Kenya. Within hours a battalion of the Lancashire Fusiliers flew in from the Canal Zone, and over a hundred prominent Africans were detained. Jomo Kenyatta, the President of the Kenya African Union, whose oratorical powers had captured

15

the hearts and imaginations of the Kikuyu, was arrested in his own home.

The Mau Mau movement, which had brought bloodshed to Kenya, was a blend of ancient and modern. It owed much to the spirit of African nationalism and the primitive trade union agitation which was growing in the towns. It owed more to witchcraft and the fear of witchcraft which flourished most strongly in the reserve. Some Mau Mau leaders wanted to destroy the white man, others wanted to uproot every vestige of European civilization. Both these elements were combined in this loosely knit movement, but as time went on the more sophisticated agitators were replaced by the men who called for the rejection of all Western ways.

It was both a strength and a weakness of Mau Mau that the movement drew its support almost exclusively from one tribe. It was for all practical purposes restricted to the Kikuyu, but the Kikuyu are the Germans of tribal Kenya. This tribe of one and a half million is noted for its devotion to education, its ability to work hard, and its intelligence. The tribal reserves, which are potentially fertile and most strategically placed, lie close to Nairobi and the European settlement areas.

In the last fifty years they had more close contact with European civilization than any other tribe in Kenya. They provided numerous clerks in Government offices, many of the most experienced hands on the European farms, and the bulk of the workers in Nairobi, the colony's capital. If they were not the colony's economic backbone, they were at least its economic pelvis. As fighting men, however, the Kikuyu were thought to be negligible. At the outbreak of the emergency only a handful were serving in the King's Rifles or the Kenya Police.

When the troubles began the congregation at many of the mission churches in the Kikuyu reserve fell by ninety per cent, and authoritative observers believe that ninety per cent of the tribe was prepared to give Mau Mau some support at some time during the emergency. Many Kikuyu were willing converts, others had to be dragged to the Mau Mau oathing ceremonies. Of all the tribes in Kenya, the Kikuyu had the greatest collective respect for the binding power of both secular and magic oaths. They had a collective passion for secret societies, and a folk affection for their traditional tribal ceremonies. These ancient oaths and ceremonies were distorted and perverted by the Mau Mau leaders. Tens of thousands of once peaceful men and women promised to kill, to cut and burn. The taking of the oaths would be solemnified with bestial ceremonies, which included the munching of human brains and intercourse with dead goats. To complete the atmosphere of horror, the 'oathing chapels' would be decorated with intestines and gouged goat's eyes.

These oaths helped to bind the bulk of the tribe together in support of Mau Mau, and to turn the tribal mind against civilization. Hundreds of Kikuyu who resisted were cut to bits, strangled or buried alive. Brother butchered brother with evident enjoyment. In theory Mau Mau was anti-white, but in practice the terrorists killed nearly a hundred times as many Africans as Europeans. During the emergency more Europeans were killed in traffic accidents within the city limits of Nairobi than were murdered by terrorists in the whole of Kenya.

The arrest of Jomo Kenyatta's colleagues deprived Mau Mau of its recognized political leaders, but this did not check the spread of terror. More British troops arrived; more battalions of the King's African Rifles were moved into the colony. The Kenya Regiment was mobilized and the Kenya police force was expanded rapidly. Loyal members of the Kikuyu were recruited into a Home Guard. The Kikuyu reserve was soon speckled with armed

posts. Real success, however, could not come quickly.
Our forces were impressive, but they had few hittable
targets. The terrorists rarely moved or operated in the
open, and hardly ever attacked any soldier or civilian who
had a chance to protect himself. By day all was usually
peaceful. By night the terrorists swept over the reserve and
settled areas, taking food, taking money and taking life.
If the security forces were often baffled by the problem of
what to do next, so were the terrorists. They had no co-
herent plan of revolt; their objective was hazy, and their
route unmarked. What to do, and where to do it? The
Mau Mau answer was to take to the forest, the traditional
hiding place of the tribe.

The main section of the Kikuyu reserve was flanked by
two huge areas of woodland, on Mount Kenya and the
Aberdares. Before the imposition of the 'Pax Britannica'
at the end of the nineteenth century these forests had
protected the Kikuyu from the depredations of the Masai
warriors, and the slave traders; in modern times it was the
customary lair of those Kikuyu who wanted to escape
from justice, and at the beginning of the emergency there
were probably three or four hundred criminals on the run
there. After the arrest of Jomo Kenyatta active Mau Mau
supporters began to trickle into the woods, and the trickle
soon became a flood of thousands. For the most part it
was the young men, of the warrior age groups, who took
to the forest, but the oldest was nearly seventy and the
youngest member of a terrorist gang ever captured was
just eleven, while twenty per cent of the forest bands were
women.

At first life for the terrorists in the forest was not too
unpleasant. Some went in carrying bundles of their most
treasured possessions. Many had brought knives and
spoons and plates and cups. Some carried mattresses and
blankets and sheets. Supplies of food came up regularly

from the reserves, while passive supporters in the towns sent up such desirable reminders of civilization as cigarettes, oil for cleaning guns, penicillin, hypodermic syringes, sulpha drugs, aspirin and matches. In the first months of the emergency, the Mau Mau discipline was so strong that a terrorist who gave his money to a courier in the forest could be almost certain of getting (in the forest) what he wanted from any shop in Nairobi. They were always short of precision weapons, but some of the gangsters showed a remarkable facility for turning out 'guns' made from odd scraps of iron piping, door bolts, rubber bands and bits of wire. Sometimes, of course, these guns would injure the firer rather than the target.

After the first few months, however, the life of the forest terrorists deteriorated. It became increasingly difficult to get food from the reserves. Then, in the summer of 1954, 'Operation Anvil' (the search of Nairobi) destroyed much of the central passive organization in Nairobi, and broke up the best supply pipe-line.

Meanwhile the troops and police were learning to operate effectively within the forest itself. The tracker teams developed phenomenal skill at following gangs and eliminated many terrorists. Then the pseudo-gang technique was developed. Surrendered terrorists were formed into gangs by young Europeans, most of whom had been born in Kenya. Dressed in rags with faces blackened by burnt cork and boot polish, these brave young men led their squads through the forest and accounted for still more gangsters. Many terrorists, impressed by the hopelessness of their existence, surrendered, Many were killed during intra-Mau Mau arguments. Many died of disease or plain hardship. Many were killed by the security forces. By mid-1955 three or four hundred forest terrorists were being elminated each month. The hardships of the forest and the shortage of ammunition shattered the fighting spirit of the gangs.

At the beginning of the emergency captured gangsters were often fat, bloated by the meat of stolen cattle. Many had watches, and some wore two suits of clothes. By the end of 1955 the captured terrorists were lean and verminous, but the bushcraft of these survivors had reached a superlative standard. When frightened they moved at staggering speed, and some gangs have been known to run seventy miles through the forest barefoot in a single day. In the words of one policeman, 'if you want to know what it is like, try running through seventy miles of blackberry patches in your socks'. As food from the reserves became more difficult to steal, the hard core were thrown back on the resources of the forest. Every edible plant was noted. Much time was spent trapping wild animals—wire from crashed R.A.F. planes made the best snares. The hungry terrorists would sometimes eat raw monkey, or meat so maggot-ridden that even the hyenas would not touch it. Wild honey was their only sweetening, and the terrorists seemed impervious to bee stings. They would eat their honeycomb with the bees still inside.

At times of crisis the terrorists would forgo even this meagre diet, and travel without food for two or three days at a time. Only one forest terrorist captured after 1955 had an ounce of spare fat on his body. Material hardship, however, made little difference to this hard core. The soft were already dead. Most of the surviving terrorists had suffered at one stage or another from pneumonia, syphilis and other diseases. Many had recovered from bullet wounds, and their recuperative power was phenomenal. Their city clothes had long since disappeared, to be replaced by jackets and trousers of animal skin, which they would not take off for a year at a time. Some wore caps which they used to pull over their faces as protection from the rain when they slept, but at least one gang had been known to sleep without blankets on the ice near the peaks of Mount Kenya. With this toughness went a remarkable ability to detect the presence of strangers, and an unusual facility for covering their tracks. Some ran for miles on their toes like ballet dancers, others ran on their heels or the sides of their feet, so that they would not leave a recognizable trail.

By the end of 1955 only fifteen hundred of these terrorists were left at large, roaming over an area of more than six thousand square miles. Ordinary methods of warfare were clearly not going to dislodge them, and they could not be left to rot. At the height of the emergency some sixty thousand Kikuyu had been confined in detention camps. At the end of 1955 they were being released at the rate of two thousand a month. Perhaps these released detainees and their colleagues in the camps would live in peace when they returned to the reserve, but perhaps they would not. The danger of a resurgence of Mau Mau remained so long as any recognized leaders were still at large. Of these leaders by far the most powerful was Dedan Kimathi.

Chapter Two

DEDAN KIMATHI

IF the Kikuyu are the Germans of tribal Kenya, Kimathi was their Hitler. Like Hitler he had to wait until the fabric of society broke around his head, but then he was able to exploit the convulsion with throbbing, burning oratory. Financial chaos and the threat of Communism gave Hitler his chance. The corruption of the Kikuyu tribal customs by Mau Mau and the flight to the forest gave Kimathi his opportunity.

On the 31st of October 1920, Kimathi Wachiuri, later baptized with the name of Dedan, was born in the Tetu location close to Nyeri, the most northerly of all Kikuyu districts, and the one that lies closest to the Aberdares and Mount Kenya.

He was an illegitimate child, but from childhood he used the name of Wachiuri, his mother's former husband, who had died some years before Kimathi's birth. Wachiuri had been rich enough to have three wives, and theirs was a large family. Kimathi's mother had two other sons and two daughters.

As his grandmother lay dying in 1931 she sent word that Kimathi was to come to her. It was a cold and misty day. Kimathi, who was then only eleven, was brought into the mud and wattle hut where the old woman lay, and received her blessing according to Kikuyu custom. She was blind and frail. She laid her hand on Kimathi's cheek, and with her last words chose him to be leader of the family, and asked that she be turned so that she would die facing his bed. Then she dipped her finger in a goat's horn of water and sprinkled the liquid on Kimathi's head.

This event made a deep impression on the boy, and stimulated the superstitious inclinations that lurk in most Kikuyu hearts. Moreover, he believed that Ngai, the traditional god of the Kikuyu tribe, had guided his grandmother's hand, and had chosen him to be the head of the whole tribe.

At about this time he began to dream. He dreamed of lands where all the cows were brown; of places in the sky where rows of people sat on wooden benches; of death being like a gate which opened and shut; of rivers running uphill; of people standing before him in white clothes with arms outstretched, and of Ngai speaking to him in his sleep. He believed everything he dreamed, and his descriptions of these dreams made old men and women turn their heads away, for they were frightened of such things.

Kimathi did not try to win the leadership of his clan or tribe by minding his manners. Long before his grandmother made her gesture he had been saddled with a reputation for delinquency. When barely out of the toddling stage he was nicknamed 'Njangu' (rough and treacherous) by his playmates.

At the age of six he went on hunger strike because his mother would not give him the sort of shield normally carried by an adolescent apprentice warrior. He killed some goats belonging to a friend of his mother with a bow and arrow. He refused to carry water for his mother. He broke his mother's maize-grinding stone. He refused to chase locusts away from the family crops, and pushed his youngest sister down an ant-bear hole. For this vindictive prank he was tied to a load of firewood by his eldest brother and flogged. Soon after his grandmother's death he slashed the nose of a bull belonging to an old man named Wachira. When he was tracked down he offered Wachira all his mother's clothes as compensation. Once he crept into a hut while all the adults were drinking native beer, and tied up the penis of a baby boy.

Fortunately for his family he was seldom at home, but he did everything possible to learn the tribal rituals and circumcision ceremonies practised by the older boys. He was certainly intelligent, but school did not have a calming effect on him. There he was brought into touch with the hot controversy that raged between the tribe and the Christian missions over female circumcision. The missionaries were doing their best to stamp out this practice as a barbaric manifestation of paganism. Many of the Kikuyu, however, regarded it as an unchangeable feature of their tribal tradition. As a by-product of this controversy a number of independent schools were started by dissident Kikuyu. Most of these soon passed into the hands of disreputable teachers, who dispensed a heady brew of anti-white, anti-government and anti-Christian dogma to their impressionable pupils.

At the age of fifteen Kimathi became a pupil at Karuni-ini school in Tetu. He was soon so good at poetry and English that his teacher gave him a goat. While he was at this school Kimathi lived with an old man, Waithangi Muthui, who paid his school fees of ninepence a month. Kimathi's progress astonished Waithangi, who soon looked on him as a member of his own family. But Kimathi could not change. He stole from Waithangi, sold his possessions, bartered his crops, and even ran him into debt. One day when Waithangi was away from home repairing fences, Kimathi broke into his hut, and took two shillings from the pocket of his raincoat. When the old man came back he discovered what had happened

and chased the boy away. Kimathi did not forgive or
forget. Waithangi was one of the first men to be murdered by Mau Mau in 1952. He was then almost eighty
years old.

To raise money for his school fees Kimathi set up a
small night school, where, every evening, he taught other
youths whatever he had learned during the day. He took
money or paraffin or soap, which he sold at the local mar-
ket. After three years he became a pupil at a more advanced school in Tetu, called Wandumbi. To meet the
higher fees he spent two days a week wandering through
the Aberdare forest collecting the seeds of Grevillia
Robusta trees, for which the Forestry Department was
then paying a penny a tin. His seed-collecting forays gave
him an early experience of forest life, which he never forgot.

Kimathi loved traditional ceremonies, but he was willing to change the ceremony to suit himself. On the 17th
of September 1938, just before he was eighteen, Kimathi
was circumcised in the dispensary at Ihururu, the administrative centre of Tetu location. The fact that he had
not been circumcised at a public ceremony according to
tribal custom was soon discovered by the other young
men, who began to laugh at him. In reply he challenged
all those who had been circumcised during the same week
to dance with him. The neighbours awaited this contest
with excitement, but when the time came all the other
young men were suffering too much to attend. To the
cheers and applause of hundreds of onlookers, Kimathi
danced alone.

In 1939 Kimathi tried his hand at working. After
getting a registration certificate from the District Commissioner, he went to the Forestry Department in Nyeri
and was hired to drive oxen hauling timber out of the
forest. After one week he was attached to a Sikh forestry

officer who was going on an expedition down the edge of the reserve to Fort Hall. Kimathi was chosen to carry the Sikh's suitcase, but once he was safely out of Nyeri he doubled back with the suitcase, and was never seen again by the Sikh or the Forestry Department.

With this ill-gotten wealth Kimathi returned to his studies. His teacher at that time was Eliud Mugo, who later became one of Mau Mau's most steadfast enemies. Closing an eye to Kimathi's misconduct, and intrigued by his capacity to learn, Eliud arranged for Kimathi's entry into the Church of Scotland Mission School at Tumu-Tumu. Apart from a break of three months early in 1941 when he joined the army, Kimathi stayed there for two years, causing trouble, refusing to pay his fees, but learning fast. He was finally expelled in February 1944.

His brief army career was not without incident. In the first week at the depot Kimathi threw some groundnuts he had been given to eat at his N.C.O. Exactly a month later he received his first pay, which he spent on native beer. A drunken brawl followed. When the military police arrived on the scene and fired over the heads of the trouble-makers, Kimathi managed to slip away unseen, and spent the next two days hiding underneath a bed in the cook's house.

After leaving Tumu-Tumu Kimathi moved from job to job. He was variously a school teacher, a dairy clerk, an employee of the Shell Company, a timber clerk and a trader in hides. But, as before, his career was chequered. He stole a bicycle from a labourer on a farm in the Naromoru district. On a farm near Thomson's Falls he beat up an old Turkana herdsman and stole his money. Then, while employed as a clerk at a farm north of Nyeri, he appropriated some money and fled north to Ol Kalou. No one seemed able to catch up with him.

In January 1949 he reappeared in the Tetu location,

and unobtrusively obtained employment as a teacher in his old school Karuna-ini. Within three months he was summoned before the school council and charged with raping two of the young girls he was teaching.

Once again he fled north to Ol Kalou, where he got a temporary job on a pig farm. There he lost the index finger on his left hand while grinding corn for the hogs.

Despite, or perhaps because of, his lack of scruples, Kimathi became a popular figure with the uneducated Kikuyu that he met during his travels. Dabbling in clandestine subversive activities by night, and posing as the future leader of the tribe by day, he gained considerable influence in the outlying areas of the central and Rift Valley provinces. At that time violence and thieving were regarded as positive virtues by the bulk of Kikuyu youth—provided that the thug or thief was successful. Kimathi was successful.

For some time past Kimathi had taken a hand at organizing the stewards who controlled the mass rallies in the reserve addressed by Jomo Kenyatta and other politicians. Kimathi and his men were there to use strong-arm tactics against any opposition, but he also listened and he learned. On the 2nd of June 1952, having already taken the Mau Mau oath twice and become a leading oath administrator in the Ol Kalou and Thomson's Falls area, he was appointed secretary of the local branch of the Kenya African Union, an organization closely interwoven with Mau Mau. Now he began to prepare for the migration into the forest which was to follow the outbreak of violence.

Four months later, having first travelled deep into the Aberdare forest with a party of young Kikuyu that included his two brothers, Wambararia and Wagura, he suddenly appeared in an area called Kanunga. Helped by several other men who were about to become leading

terrorists, he organized a massive Mau Mau oath ceremony on the banks of the Gura river. Thousands of Kikuyu came to it. That day, on Kimathi's express instructions, or at least with his full approval, the senior chief of
the Nyeri district, Nderi Wangombe, was brutally hacked
to death as he walked down to the river to see what was
going on.

Kimathi was now formally identified by his tribal
leaders as one of the leading oath administrators, and a
hue and cry began. He was traced to a friend's house in
his own location and there, late one night, a party of
Kikuyu tribal guards surrounded him. He was asleep, and
woke to hear them knocking at the door. For some minutes he did not answer, then as the door was being forced,
he tried to escape through the window. A guard grabbed
him, handcuffed him and took him off to the chief's
camp at Ihururu. At the camp Kimathi recognized one
of the chief's assistants as a Mau Mau supporter. When
the other guards had gone the supporter returned and the
two men bargained. Kimathi offered his bicycle in exchange for freedom. The bargain was struck. The cell
door was unlocked, and Kimathi disappeared in the darkness. He was off to the Aberdares.

At the time that he walked out of the cell Dedan
Kimathi was thirty-two and untested. His educational
attainments were pitifully small by Western standards,
but they were substantial in comparison with those of his
fellow Kikuyu. He could add and subtract, and divide
and multiply—if the numbers were not too large. He
could write and read English a bit. At one time he showed
a liking for American paper-backed cowboy stories and
thrillers, but he had to struggle with the words, and it
seems their lurid covers were the principal attraction.
The British withdrawal from India had a profound effect
on Kimathi, and he was aware also of the Egyptian ter-

rorist activities in the Canal Zone. He knew of the existence of the Soviet Union, but the theory of Communism and the subtleties of dialectical materialism meant nothing to him. He did, however, know the Bible as accurately as many a lay preacher. At times he seemed to believe that the Bible had been written especially for him. He carried an Old Testament translated into Kikuyu wherever he went. He spoke in parables, and his harangues were larded with allusions to and quotations from the Bible. As an orator he was magnetic, compelling, irresistible. In the rest of Kenya there were a few Africans who could have held their own with Kimathi in council or on the platform. But they were not in the forest and Kimathi was.

He also had a plan, or at least the glimmerings of one. As bemused recruits poured into the forest, Kimathi would assign them to gangs and appoint leaders. From time to time he would regroup his forces, and these reorganizations were complex affairs involving as many as two thousand men. He adopted British ranks, and the orderly room terminology of the British Army. When Kimathi had fled to the Aberdares he took with him a pencil, notebook and some carbon paper. Now Kimathi wrote out his *Mien Kampf*, telling his men how they would take over the European farms; how they would kill all those—black, white or brown—who stood against them. These pages were torn from a notebook and passed around the gangs. These odd sheets of paper were the sum total of Mau Mau literature in the forest, and they added immensely to Kimathi's reputation. No one now doubted his authority in the land of the trees.

He formed two main councils, which he called the Nyandarua Defence Council and the Gikuyu na Mumbi Itungati Association. The first was to formulate policy and appoint leaders for the gangs, the second would pre-

pare the rank and file for the life of violence that now lay
before them. He welcomed the steady destruction of all
links with civilization, and as his men forgot their past
they worshipped their leader with increased fervour.

His followers were certain he had the power to alter
the course of rivers, to transform the ranching lands of
the European farmers into lakes of stagnant water, and
to lead the Mau Mau on to certain victory.

In this exalted position death was his to command.
He was the invincible ruler of the mountains, and no one
could speak to him without his express permission. He
dreamed dreams in which he saw himself as the King of
Africa or the 'popular Prime Minister of the Southern
Hemisphere'. At a public ceremony deep in the jungle
he bestowed himself with the title 'K.C.A.E.' to signify
that he had been appointed, 'by God', a Knight Commander of the African Empire. After that he called himself 'Prime Minister Sir Dedan Kimathi'.

For a long time he enjoyed life in the jungle, where he
lived in undisputed comfort. He found luxuries he had
never seen before. He was protected by many devoted
terrorists whom he had specially selected; he was enter-
tained by young Kikuyu girls abducted from the Kikuyu
reserve. He was waited on by countless Kikuyu youngsters
who held high hopes that when the end he predicted became a reality, they would live a lifetime of luxurious
pleasure. He chose for himself, or was given without asking, all the more valuable or useful items of property
stolen on Mau Mau raids.

He made it his personal concern to see that no other
terrorist achieved sufficient popularity to become a com-
petitor for his supreme position. There were a few who,
by demonstrating a particular ferocity at the time of Mau
Mau raids, or by showing special qualities of leadership,
gained too much popularity for his liking. These he

'demoted' and stripped of their followers, and sent to distant areas where they could not endanger his authority. If they dissented, or if they came back, he would have them strangled with a rope and left for the hyenas to eat. His two brothers, who entered the forest with him, Wambararia and Wagura, lived a precarious life. It was often said by his men that had his brothers not been 'from the same womb as he was himself' he would have done away with them. These two derived some popularity in the forest from their relationship with Kimathi and there was always a tendency among the Mau Mau rank and file to treat them with a degree of respect and care which those unrelated to Kimathi did not enjoy. When Kimathi realized this he foresaw the possibility that they might in time gain enough popularity to unseat him. From that moment he made a point of keeping both of them well under his heel, never allowing them to participate in any affairs which might bring them into the limelight. Wagura was shot and killed in the forest in 1954. When news of this was brought to Kimathi by one of his subordinate leaders, he remarked, 'Tell me the names of others who were killed, but never mention the names of my brothers.' After Wagura's death Wambararia became one of Kimathi's servants, and for the next two years his sole task was to cook food for his brother. He was fat, for as cook he very properly made a point of looking after himself, but the task carried no prestige, and Wambararia, who had all the makings of a terrorist leader nearly as dangerous as his brother, never rose to any level of importance.

But these good times were not to last for Kimathi. As the initiative was wrested from the Mau Mau, as more and more of his fanatical followers fell to the army, the police and the Kikuyu loyalists, he found he could no longer convene mass meetings in the forest and stand before thousands of excited worshippers. No longer was he able to live in the comfort of rainproof shelters and sleep on a wooden bed, with ample blankets sent up to him by supporters in the native reserves, nor did he receive new clothes and medicines from Nairobi.

His organization began to lose its cohesion, and the time soon came when he did not know where to find his subordinates, or even whether they were dead or alive. His control over the once large organization of terrorists had always been fairly remote, now he lost touch with all but a few of the gangs. The 'passive wing' of Mau Mau, the mass of Kikuyu in the native areas, in the towns and on the farms, who had taken the oath and who supplied the 'militant wing' with arms, food, clothing, medicine and information, was gradually broken up by the Security Forces. Kimathi was thus cut off from the outside world. Furthermore, the forest gangs found their raids becoming progressively more dangerous, costly in casualties and unproductive of booty. Kimathi, like everyone else, had to live off the land.

The effect of all this upon Kimathi was profound. He unleashed his fury, not on the terrorists who were guarding him, for he could not do without them, but on those who had 'betrayed the community' by committing minor infringements of his rules. Eating food before it had been shared out, speaking in his presence without his permission, sleeping with women, failing to pray to Ngai; these and thirty-four other lesser deeds all resulted in the death of the offender. The terrorists from the Fort Hall district were the ones who suffered most from his tantrums. He found fault with almost everything they did or did not do, and strangled them in large numbers. Nothing pleased him more than to stand in the forest as the 'Mutui wohoro' or the Dictator of Justice, and see his followers' blood flow. Those who were with him at this

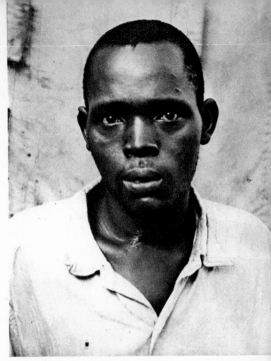

GENERAL CHINA

P.A.-Reuter

GENERAL CHINA

Camera Press

MOUNT KENYA

Dept. of Information, Nairobi

time have said that these executions became his sole amusement, and he arranged them as frequently as his own security would permit. This reaction, not unprecedented among megalomaniacs in times of imminent defeat, became more pronounced as events became worse. He soon gained the reputation in the jungle of being the most dangerous killer of them all. What some others thought of him is summed up in the words of a surrendered terrorist from Fort Hall, who said, 'Nobody has helped the Government as much as Kimathi, and for that reason he should be given a salary. He has killed more Mau Mau than any member of the Security Forces.' Of that there was no doubt.

By the end of 1955 Kimathi's life was drastically different from what it had been in 1953 or 1954. Killing was his sole interest, and as he never found the opportunity of killing outside his mountain domain, he killed lavishly within it. He was always thinking about pseudogangs. It infuriated him to think that some of those who had taken the powerful oaths of the Mau Mau, and who had once idolized and worshipped him, had surrendered and then come back to hunt him and his followers. Knowing that this had happened in some cases, he believed it could happen in every case, and he hated everyone.

Of his original harem he only kept one woman, Wanjiru, a nineteen-year-old Kikuyu girl from his own district of Nyeri. All the others he strangled.

Yet he and his henchmen adapted themselves to the privations and hardships of isolation in the forest with great success. In this cruel reversion to an animal existence, Kimathi outstripped all the others. As he learnt more about the forest he forgot more about civilization. He chewed skins and bones like a hyena; his eyes flicked about like those of a nervous monkey; he would only

B

drink water as a buck or a goat drinks, by lowering his head to it; he never washed, and his lice-ridden hair grew down his shoulders until it was long enough for him to use as a swat for horseflies. All the time, day and night, he was on the alert, and his powers of sight, hearing and smell grew abnormally acute.

He had never been a brave man. Every terrorist who knew him well will confirm that he was one of the most timid of all those who entered the forest. Even when he was at the height of his power he ran no risks. But now he was cowardly in the extreme. This did not disturb his henchmen, however, for in their estimation 'a leader appointed by Ngai', chosen from among thousands to lead them in the forest, and blessed by an old woman, did not have to be brave. They knew that with his instinct and intuition and their courage and determination they had little to fear. His existence was therefore dependent upon them, and theirs upon him, and particularly upon his inexplicable ability to sense danger. Within one month of entering the forest in 1952 he chose his personal guard. It never numbered more than sixty-one. Three years later fifty of them were still with him.

Yet despite his powerful bodyguard, despite his understanding of the jungle, his wariness and his temperament, his main shield of defence was undoubtedly his reputation. Everyone, both inside and outside the forest, knew how dangerous he was. Nothing was more disturbing than the thought of falling into his hands. Some of his followers may have come to hate him, but if this was so their hate was never apparent. It was submerged in an abyss of terror, terror of Kimathi as an individual and terror of his reputed connection with Ngai, the supreme deity whose home according to Kikuyu mythology was the snow-capped peak of Mount Kenya.

Kimathi, in the words of one policeman, 'was as elusive as a butterfly'. But if the myth of Mau Mau was going to be broken once and for all, this poison butterfly would have to be caught.

Chapter Three

KINYANJUI

WHILE the future terrorist leader was being blessed by
his grandmother, Kimathi's principal opponent, Ian Henderson, was toddling about in his nursery just a few miles
further north. A few years before the First World War, Jock
Henderson, Ian's father, had been sent out to Kenya by
an enterprising firm of Scottish merchants. This visionary
scheme for starting a flourishing seed trade on Kenya's
fertile soil came to nothing, but Jock Henderson stayed
on. He liked the climate; he liked the space; he liked the
pioneering atmosphere. He looked for gold, and did not
find it. He took part in the guerilla campaigns in German
East Africa. He grew sisal at Thika and he married a
friend from Scotland whose experiences with snakes and
wild animals in those early days were hair-raising. They
took to cattle farming, and were nearly ruined when a
visiting Swede quietly sold six hundred of their cattle and
decamped with the money. Then the family moved on
to a coffee farm just outside the small town of Nyeri.
Their farm, which stretched almost from the township
line to the edge of the Aberdares, ran up to the best game
forest in Kenya. The well-known Treetops game lookout
was built a few hundred yards from the farm's boundary
fence. The view was superb—impressive but friendly.
Mount Kenya rose a few miles to the east and the Aberdares a few hundred yards to the west. From the farm-
house you could watch the smoke rising from huts in the
Kikuyu reserve, but there were not many white neigh-

bours in sight. Sometimes the family's European friends
and neighbours would come up for a rumbustious tennis
party, which spilled over the acres of lawn. Sometimes
there would be parties at other houses, or at the club.
Sometimes Jock Henderson would decide to take his
family, and his African farm hands, into town for a Sunday celebration, and the party would sweep into Nyeri,
singing and laughing, on the family lorry. But it could
have been a lonely life for a farmer's young son; there
were no white playmates nearby for young Ian, but there
were plenty of African boys on the farm, and Ian played
with them.

So young Henderson formed and led his first band
of Africans. He was the warrior leader, not a distant
white king in a distant white house. He played with them.
He talked with them. He fought and thought with them.
And he always asked questions.

Then there was the forest. Sometimes he went in alone,
sometimes he led groups of African youngsters in a search
for butterflies. Sometimes, as he grew older, they looked
for more substantial game. By the time he was approaching adolescence, young Henderson was a first-class shot,
and he was able to get plenty of practice. There were a
dozen guns in the house.

At the age of eleven Ian had his first ride on a motor-
bicycle. His legs were not long enough to reach the foot
controls, which were operated by a slightly larger
Kikuyu youth perched behind him on the saddle. This
example of black/white co-operation did not last very
long. They crashed, and Henderson still carries a formidable scar on his thigh. During the Mau Mau troubles
his former playmate was sentenced to seven years' imprisonment for cutting the legs off a farmer's cows.

The farm and the forest were the strongest material
influence on Ian Henderson's youth. At school in Nairobi

he did well enough in School Certificate, with distinctions in French and Art. He was good at rugger, and hockey, and cricket, and long-distance running; he was a lance-corporal in the school cadet force. It was a creditable, if not an outstanding, record. The Prince of Wales School did something to broaden his mind, but his ambition still centred on a quiet agricultural life. For a time his father thought of sending him to a forestry school in New Zealand, but the war was still flickering on. The fighting would clearly be over by the time he was trained, and it looked as though military service would mean nothing but a dull round of garrison duty in Germany or Japan.

In Kenya, however, there was an alternative to military service. He could join the police, and he did so in February 1945, just before his eighteenth birthday. In his first training tour he scrubbed down the cells slept in by African drunks, and from this he graduated to the almost equally unpleasant job of traffic officer for Nairobi, a city notorious for sticky traffic jams, inadequate parking spaces and bad driving.

Every police force in the world, however, is short of men with a talent for detective work, and young Henderson soon moved from bicycle thefts to armed robbery and murder. It was an interesting career, though he still hankered after country life, and at one point he left the police to help his father on the farm. He was an ordinary young Kenyan, fond of sport, popular with his colleagues, meticulously neat, interested in things rather than ideas, and not much given to theorizing about the meaning of the European presence in Africa. But he had one extraordinary qualification, he knew the Kikuyu people and he knew their language. He knew how their minds worked, and he knew where to go to get information. This was of vital importance even in ordinary police work. When he was still a junior officer eighteen houses were broken into at Nanyuki, a town not far from Nyeri. The local police could find no conclusive clues. Henderson was sent for. Within a fortnight he had solved fifteen of the robberies.

This knowledge of the Kikuyu was still more valuable when he was transferred to Special Branch. At last he was the proverbial round peg in the round hole, but the months that followed were pure frustration. His African friends were going bad before his eyes. When Princess Elizabeth came to Kenya in 1952 he commanded her guard at Sagana Lodge, but most of the time he just had to watch and to worry.

Then the emergency began and frustration was left behind. Only a handful of Europeans could speak Kikuyu fluently and at last he was able to act. Jomo Kenyatta was still a key figure, idolized by the tribe, the only Kikuyu with an international reputation. While many suspected what his real role in the foundation of Mau Mau had been, the case still remained to be proved in an open court. There was little doubt that Kenyatta would be convicted if the witnesses for the prosecution would testify, but would they run the risk involved? Every African witness knew that he was only too likely to lose his life, or his tongue, or his hands, to Mau Mau revenge squads. The preparation of the case against Kenyatta, with the protection of the Government's witnesses, was Henderson's first front-rank assignment. The Government witnesses all gave their evidence and Jomo Kenyatta was convicted and sentenced to seven years' imprisonment. He was whisked away to the North Frontier district. The figurehead of the Mau Mau had been cut off but the body and limbs lived on.

The next few months were hectic. There were too few trained police officers and all were overworked. There

was also a substantial element of risk. On the night of the
Lari massacre, when two hundred Kikuyu men, women
and children were cut down by Mau Mau terrorists, he
was ambushed and his car set on fire. In the words of
one of his African assistants, 'Mr. Henderson does not
work with time,' and at weekends, when many of his
friends were off playing golf, he would leave his attractive,
patient wife at home with their baby daughter and plunge
into the forests of Mount Kenya to look for General
China, the principal Mau Mau leader in that part of the
world. His reward was a bullet through his left arm.

On the 16th of January 1954 General China did fall
into the Government's hands. Ian Henderson was his
principal interrogator—and General China decided to
co-operate. Securing the co-operation of General China
was a substantial achievement, but this was only the
beginning of a curious chapter. The terrorists in the
forests of Mount Kenya had to be persuaded to obey
their former leader and give up terrorism. An involved
series of meetings and confrontations now took place.

In the words of the citation of his first George Medal:
'Between February 13 and April 10, 1954, Mr Henderson
was in immediate command of the Special Branch de-
tachment assigned the duty of attempting to bring about
a meeting between Government representatives and
those of the terrorists in the Mount Kenya area. The
nature of this assignment made it necessary for Mr.
Henderson to travel frequently into the forests and parts
of the reserves occupied by terrorists under conditions of
extreme vulnerability in order to achieve the objective.'
These official words mean that Henderson walked into
the forest time after time—often unarmed—to parley
with a band of half-crazed thugs. Slowly he climbed the
Mau Mau ladder of command, meeting leaders of in-
creasing importance at each successive step. The

negotiations were protracted, and the conditions were trying. Whenever Henderson or his colleagues reached into their pockets for a cigarette or a handkerchief, the terrorist leaders would suspect a trap and grab their weapons.

Henderson led his party into the forest and talked for the Government. He alone knew both the thickets of the forest and the thickets of the terrorist mind.

A military mishap for which a stray band of Mau Mau were responsible broke the confidence of the terrorists just at the moment when it seemed that they would surrender in large numbers, but these negotiations confirmed Ian Henderson's reputation with both the Government and the terrorists. In the words of the Governor, Sir Evelyn Baring, 'a number of people were giving us advice on what the Mau Mau would do next. No one was right the whole time, but Ian Henderson was right more often than anyone else.'

The terrorists also respected him. The Kikuyu give everyone nicknames and Henderson was called 'Kinyanjui' after a Gladstonian elder statesman of the tribe who had died just before the first world war. The name Kinyanjui was not merely symbolic. Traditionally the Kikuyu respect the advice of their elders. The power of the generation is of vital importance. It is not based on official position but is founded on the respect which Africans normally accord to age and experience. The angry young men of Mau Mau had thrust the elders aside, but now these angry young men were in the forest and doing very badly. Violence had not been a success. Thousands were dead and tens of thousands were interned. The tribe was being hurt and the elders were speaking out. Ian Henderson knew the elders and knew what they were saying. When he sat huddled up in a forest clearing arguing away in the terrorist patois, which he had to

B*

learn during the talks, he spoke not only for the white man's Government but also for the elders of the tribe.

By 1955 the Mau Mau front was beginning to crack badly. Henderson played his part in the development of the pseudo-gang technique, and then went into the forest of the Aberdares for the 'Chui' surrender talks, where he earned his second George Medal. Once again Henderson was the spokesman for the Government. Once again it took weeks to climb the ladder of leaders. But this time he knew that Kimathi was opposed to the talks and was trying to sabotage them, and clearly the best way to sabotage them would be to cut off Henderson's head. The talks began to the noise of crackling explosions as certain gas-filled bamboo shoots popped in the sunlight after the rains. They failed when Kimathi seized the principal terrorists taking part. Kimathi was implacable, but many of the other leaders seemed to enjoy talking. They knew that they were isolated, and they did not all like losing touch with their families and the main body of the tribe. As Commissioner Richard Catling, who has a distinguished record of Special Branch work himself, said, 'Ian was just about the only window I had on the Mau Mau mind.' Henderson was also the last window through which the terrorists could look at the outside world. Kinyanjui was their last telephone wire, their last link with the Government, their last link with civilization.

This new eminence did not shake Ian Henderson's diffident manner. Even his hair seems to recede out of modesty. His slim, wiry body seeks the background, but his eyes are memorable.

When discussing his own specialities, however, he has abundant self-confidence. To a direct question he will give an exhaustive reply, and assume that everyone from the Governor downwards will listen to the whole answer.

He combines the true Kikuyu's circuitous approach to a difficult problem with a policeman's reluctance to share his secrets. He is too gregarious to be the complete lone wolf but he works best on the longest of long reins. He is an individualist with an unusual combination of quirks and qualities, and an unusual charm.

He is patient but volatile. He is exceptionally practical —the administration of his operations was always first class—but he could grasp and sometimes mould the mad theories of the Mau Mau. He has immense stamina, immense physical and mental energy, but he is highly strung. Sometimes when driving down to Nairobi from the forest he was known to roar with laughter because of the release from tension. His neat bungalow on the outskirts of Nairobi is almost antiseptically clean, but in the forest he often had to huddle under some louse-laden blanket with his terrorists.

Perhaps there is a touch of masochism to be found in all long-distance runners, and Henderson is no exception. Of one tense moment he has written: 'It was the same feeling one had as a child when knocking on the headmaster's door for a caning—a nice feeling in many ways because it was exciting, gripping and different from the dull routine of one's everyday life.'

It is certainly difficult to imagine how Henderson could have survived the mental and physical strain without a certain enjoyment of discomfort for discomfort's sake. But allied with this ability to withstand and even enjoy the onslaughts of nature and mankind is a fierce Scottish pride, a love of the British Empire and a stern devotion to his own Kenya.

As Lieutenant-General Sir Gerald Lathbury said in his farewell message to Special Branch, 'Ian Henderson has probably done more than any single individual to bring the emergency to an end.'

Certainly few white men in the history of British Africa had shown such ability to understand and manipulate a tribal mentality. Would he be equally successful with the hard core? Would he be able to manipulate the fanatics?

Kinyanjui, 'the elder statesman', and his Special Branch colleagues now turned their full attention to the problem of catching Kimathi.

Chapter Four

A PLAN IS MADE

BY the end of 1955 only a handful of terrorists were being captured each week. The fifteen hundred still at large were the bushcraft experts, and as their numbers dwindled the survivors were harder to find in the six thousand square mile forest of the Aberdares. Even the pseudo-gang leaders were for the most part having little success. These pseudo-gangs were largely made up of ex-terrorists who had surrendered. They were, inevitably, less tough, less primitive, than the hard core in the forest. They had surrendered because they could not take it. Even the best of the pseudo-terrorists would soon lose their edge—that uncanny sensitivity which life in the jungle had given them. They developed a taste for the good food they saw others eating. They wanted to sleep in warm beds between blankets. They wanted clothes to shield them from the rain and cold. They wanted to drive as far as they could into the forest before taking to their feet. They wanted injections 'to wash the blood' when they felt ill. Above all they developed a feeling for safety, and with this sense of safety they lost their understanding of the forest.

Finally, inevitably, the remaining Mau Mau soon realized that former terrorists were being used to hunt them. They now took special precautions against the pseudos. Most of the surviving hard core knew all their colleagues by sight. New faces, they had learnt, were dangerous. No form of disguise, however perfect, was now good enough. The chances of catching Dedan

45

Kimathi with an ordinary pseudo-gang were remote. The intelligence experts had little information about him. He and his bodyguard generally avoided meeting other gangs. He had long since stopped his own foragers and raiders leaving the forest to pillage European farms. He did not want his men to expose themselves, and in this he was highly successful.

It was virtually certain that he was in the Aberdares, but that information was not much comfort to Kimathi's hunters. The Aberdares rise fairly steeply from the plains of the Central Province, and then at eleven thousand feet it looks as if the whole top of the mountain has been cut away with a jagged saw. The flat top, known as the Moorlands, is eighty miles long. It is a place of swamps, lakes, icy winds and swirling mists. Towards the middle of the Moorlands there is a great depression in the land. Here the lakes get bigger, the cold water seeps slowly through the tufty grass which bubbles and oozes when you step on it. Immediately below the Moorlands stands the bamboo belt. This is approximately twelve to fifteen miles wide and circles the whole mountain, covering an area of some four thousand square miles. The old bamboo has been blown over, and the remains make a thick tangled mattress of dried poles. Through this layer new shoots have grown up. In some places it is so thick that only a faint glimmer of light can be seen when the sun is directly overhead at mid-day. This tangled interwoven mass, which stands twenty-five feet high, made an ideal hiding place for the terrorists, but the tropical bamboo is a treacherous growth. Its thin sharp leaves can cut your skin like a razor, and as the wind blows on the leaves a shower of invisible bamboo hair will fall on your skin and cause severe itching, while the sharp pointed shoots and sticks are a constant menace to the travellers' eyes. Below the bamboo belt there is yet another belt of deci-

duous 'black' forest. This belt is extremely thick in
parts, and it is often difficult to see more than three
or four feet ahead. But it is easier and quieter to move
through than the bamboo.

Faced with the massive problem of finding the terrorist needle in this vast haystack of a mountain, an
expert committee of three was set up. There was Assistant
Commissioner John Prendergast, G.M., the Director of
Special Branch, and a veteran of the last forest surrender talks. This tall, handsome Irishman, who worked
before the war for the Middlesex County Council, had
built up a distinguished record of intelligence work in
Palestine, Port Said and the Gold Coast. The second
member was Superintendent Anthony Lapage, a square,
solid, smiling man, whose father had been bailiff on the
Duke of Wellington's estate in Hampshire. When Tony
Lapage came to Kenya before the last war, he had turned
from farming to the forest. There he had hunted for
bumblebee mice; he had hunted for the elusive spotted
lion of Kenya. More recently he had hunted for Mau
Mau with substantial success. The third member of the
committee was Ian Henderson.

They reviewed the numerous operations that had been
launched during the past three years in an effort to catch
Kimathi. Thousands of soldiers and policemen had taken
part. There had been sweeping operations, cordon operations, operations to starve him into the open country,
intelligence schemes designed to attract him towards
bogus sources of supply. There had even been psychological operations with coloured smoke and recorded voices in
the night. These schemes had been ingenious and were
carried out with skill, but they did not work. There was
no obvious way of catching Kimathi, only improbable
schemes had a chance of success, and the committee
chose the most improbable.

They would try to seize some members of Kimathi's gang. They would try to convert the gangsters before Kimathi missed them, and they would try to persuade the gangsters to lead a striking force back to Kimathi. The odds against success were clearly enormous. The whole plan was drenched with complications. How could contact be made with the gang? How could gangsters be captured without Kimathi's knowledge? How could they be made to co-operate quickly? Unless there was a solution to all these problems the effort would be wasted.

The mere fact that this preposterous plan was backed by the Commissioner of Police, Mr. Richard Catling, and the Commander-in-Chief, Lieutenant-General Sir Gerald Lathbury, was ample proof that everything within reason had already been tried and found wanting.

First the committee had to make contact with Kimathi's men. How would they do it? They would write the gang a letter. The problem of contact in the forest worried the Mau Mau as well as the security forces. Our troops had wireless sets, but the Mau Mau could only write letters to each other. With stubby pencils on grubby paper they scribbled notes for each other, which they posted in their letter boxes. These letter boxes, known only to their friends, would be holes in trees, cracks in rocks, or other places hard to see.

Henderson and his colleagues decided that three identical letters should be written by a surrendered terrorist, and posted in three separate parts of the forest. The letters would call on the gang to surrender. Previous experience gained in writing letters to Mau Mau leaders urging them to surrender had shown that if you mentioned any specific terrorist leader by name in a letter there would be no response. The individual concerned would feel that a special trap was being set for him, and

he would go out of his way to persuade everyone in the
forest to ignore the letter. Kimathi would not be mentioned in these new letters, they would be addressed to
'The People in the Forest', but it was hoped that any
such letter found in the forest would find its way up the
ladder to Kimathi.

After the letters had been posted an aircraft fitted
with a powerful loudspeaker would fly over the forest,
sky-shouting a recorded message announcing the position of the letters. The leaders would not go to the letter
point themselves, but if their curiosity were aroused they
might well send one or two of their followers to collect
the message. The sky-shouted message had to arouse their
curiosity, and had to say where the letters were posted,
but it had to avoid giving much indication of the contents of the letters, otherwise the gangsters would not
bother to collect them at all. If Dedan Kimathi had not
actually heard the sky shout himself he would soon be
told about it. A conference would be called. Kimathi
would preside, and some junior terrorists would be sent
off to collect one of the letters.

Provided Henderson and his colleagues could capture
these terrorists, indirect contact with Kimathi would
have been made. They then developed a plan for capturing the messengers. The ambushers might have to remain hidden, motionless and silent, for days on end, as
no one could say when the letters would be collected, if
they were collected at all. However long it took the messengers to arrive, the ambush party would have to strike
so quickly that no one could escape. The escape of a
single terrorist would jeopardize the whole venture.
Once the messengers had been captured Henderson and
his colleagues felt reasonably confident that they would
be able to get the terrorists' co-operation. Every interrogator has his technique for handling an unwilling

criminal, and Special Branch had had some notable successes.

At this point Tony Lapage and Ian Henderson went round to talk to a number of ex-terrorists now enrolled in pseudo-gangs, to hear what they had to say about the plan. Most of them agreed that curiosity would drive Kimathi to send someone to collect one of the letters, but no one believed that any of the terrorists in the forest would willingly betray their supreme leader. In their view Henderson would not even have a chance to try to win their co-operation. There would be a heated gun battle, they thought, as soon as the ambush was sprung, and the messengers would fight to the death.

Two more problems remained before the plan could be put into action. Where should the letters be planted, and where should the warning message be sky-shouted? Henderson and Lapage now went to various detention camps to talk to terrorists who had just come from the forest. No one had seen Kimathi for weeks, but they did discover that in the earlier stages of the emergency Kimathi had shown a peculiar liking for three particular spots on the eastern slopes of the Aberdares. Perhaps he was still there. They then looked for three suitable areas in the region where the letters could be planted. This was far from easy. The points had to be suitable for ambush, they had to be points which could be described in detail within six seconds, the absolute time limit for any sky-shouting message. There would not be time for elaborate descriptions before the aircraft flew out of hearing range.

For a time the committee thought about abandoning the sky-shouter system and dropping leaflets instead, but the cost would have been considerable, and Mau Mau had come to regard all leaflets as nothing more than 'rubbish to mislead' them. The use of pamphlets would get the scheme off to a bad psychological start.

Finally Henderson and his colleagues picked three points, which were so well known to the terrorists that they had been given terrorist nicknames. The first of these was an old Mau Mau hideout used by Dedan Kimathi in 1953. In those days it had been the site for many important terrorist meetings, and was known to the Mau Mau as Mihuro, meaning at the bottom, or the seat of their deliberations. Everyone knew where Mihuro was. The second point was a large Mau Mau food store, long abandoned, on the slopes of a small hill known as Karathi's Mother. Many years ago, according to Kikuyu legend, a Kikuyu woman had sacrificed her only son, Karathi, at the top of this hill in the hope that evil spirits would be appeased and that the locusts eating her crops would vanish. The other point was an enormous rock weighing some five tons at the end of Wanderers' Track. Dedan Kimathi had once been able to convince his gullible followers that he had put the rock there himself to stop the Royal Engineers building the track further up the mountain. The terrorists implicitly believed this ridiculous story, and his achievement was soon discussed through the forest. Whenever Mau Mau gangs were nearby they visited the rock and marvelled at Kimathi's superhuman powers.

How could Henderson and his colleagues best ambush these points? They approached the police and army dog teams, but none of the dog handlers could guarantee that their animals would remain silent for long in the forest. They considered using pit snares, trip wires and other obstacles, but there was no real alternative to the use of a small number of handpicked police. But could anyone be counted on to remain alert if a terrorist messenger did not come for four or five days? It was decided to change tactics. Instead of ambushing all three letter points, the police would keep out of the forest until Henderson and Lapage discovered that a letter had been removed. Then, before the terrorists had time to bring back their reply, they would move up and ambush that particular point.

This now meant that all three letters had to be so written that Kimathi would be sufficiently interested to reply. In normal circumstances Mau Mau would never reply to a letter written by a surrendered terrorist unless the writer said something about defeat. Any suggestion that defeat was imminent so infuriated the terrorists that they would, given an opportunity, seek to disillusion the author by murdering him. The letters were written in a provocatively defeatist vein, saying that the people in the forest were doomed, and that the writer would return to the same point in the jungle alone and unarmed some days later to lead the gangs into captivity. This sort of letter, it was thought, would annoy Kimathi so much that he would send some of his henchmen to kill the writer at the letter point. Seven days after the letters were planted—so went the message—the writer would return. This would give the gangs time to react to the sky-shout, collect the letter and choose the murder party.

Henderson and Lapage would plant the letters at Mihuro on the 19th of December 1955, at Karathi's Mother on the 20th, and at the rock on Wanderers' Track on the 21st. The sky-shouting would be carried out on the following days. Three days after the planting of the letters they would go back into the forest to see if any had been removed. If a letter had gone they would return again on the seventh day to await all comers. Henderson and his colleagues first had to find a needle in a haystack, and when they found it they had to persuade it to melt.

PART TWO

THE HUNT
(as told by Ian Henderson)

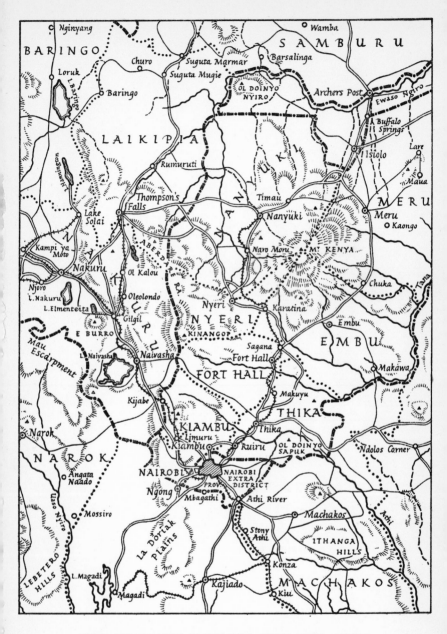

MAP SHOWING NAIROBI AND THE AREA
MAINLY AFFECTED BY THE MAU MAU

Chapter Five

UNHAPPY CHRISTMAS

Njeterera ndekinyaga

He who hesitates never arrives.

AT midnight on the 18th of December 1955, Tony
Lapage, my African Inspector Gethieya Ndirango and I
left for the Aberdares. We had made the same journey
into the forest often before, and as we drove along the
road, threading our way through the scattered Kikuyu
villages which lie below the mountain, I thought much
about Gethieya.

He had been a Kenya policeman for fourteen years,
and had worked with me for eleven of them. As Mau
Mau swept through the Kikuyu tribe, striking terror into
the lives of these normally peaceful people, he knew that
he had become an important target, for he too was a
Kikuyu. But if anything the threats to his life and family
spurred him on to greater efforts. For his exploits in the
forest he had been awarded the Colonial Police Medal
for Gallantry. Month after month, year after year, he
had battled against terrorism. And now here he was sitting between Tony and myself, ready to start all over
again. As we sped along the dusty, bumpy road, he was
half asleep with his feet up on the dashboard. When I
dug him in the ribs and asked him how he was, he gave
his stock answer: 'On the pig's back, sir.' How he loved
that phrase! Good old Gethieya!

At Nyeri, a hundred miles north of Nairobi in the

55

saddle between Mount Kenya and the Aberdares, we
picked up three African police constables who were to
guard the Land Rover. Then as dawn was breaking we
entered the Aberdare forest at Njogu-ini. There was not
a cloud in the sky as we bumped along towards the top
of the twelve thousand feet high range. Before reaching
the bamboo belt we stopped for a few minutes to have
some hot coffee from a flask. How fresh and alive it all
was! The sun rising over the shoulder of Mount Kenya
was warm and comforting. The air was strong and sweet-
smelling. The song of a hundred birds promised a beautiful morning.

As we drove higher up the track we passed elephant
footprints and rhino droppings, but apart from an occa-
sional Jackson's francolin that would suddenly dart onto the track just in front of the wheels of the Land Rover,
the journey continued without incident.

Towards mid-day we were high up the Aberdares and
could look back down the long falling slopes of the mountain to Nyeri, some thirty miles away. We were getting
close to Mihuro, our first letter-point. Finally we stopped.
Quietly we told the African constables to sit tight, and
prepared to set off through the forest. I led the way as I
had been to Mihuro before. We made no attempt to
conceal our tracks because we knew that any attempt to
hide our route might make the terrorists think we were
interested in tricking them and trapping them. If we
went in the open they would be less suspicious.

At the best of times it is a difficult journey. In this
particularly thick part of the forest you have to crawl
along the ground, climb on your hands and knees over
fallen poles and branches, walk along the stronger bamboo like a tight-rope dancer and thread your way across
patches of dry bamboo which may hide deep pits. The
shoots cut at our hands and legs and faces. Mihuro was

only three miles from the spot where we left our Land
Rover. But it took us nearly four hours to get there. We
set to work immediately. Beside one of three dilapidated
bamboo shelters which had once housed the Mau Mau
'Houses of Parliament', we scraped an area of ground
about five feet square until the bare, brown earth was
plainly visible. In the centre of this we put a thin bamboo stake and, after placing our letter inside an empty
bottle to keep it safe from the weather, we slipped the
bottle over the stake, open end downwards.

We then plotted the various places where we planned
to lie in wait, if and when our letter was removed. At
least we were sure that no terrorist could approach the
bottle through the tangle of branches without making a
noise that we were bound to hear. After that we returned
to the clearing. We knew the Mau Mau were so nervy
and suspicious that if they saw the smallest root or stick
jutting out of the ground beside the bottle, they would
imagine that a booby trap had been set for them there.
For the last time we examined the ground before starting the return journey. We now had to travel uphill all
the way, an experience well worth avoiding in this type
of country and at this altitude.

From the moment we left the Land Rover on the out-
ward journey we realized that we might well be seen by
Mau Mau sentries somewhere along the route. In order
not to look dangerous, therefore, we carried no firearms.
Our only weapons were a 36-fragmentation grenade each
in our pockets. As we climbed we were thinking of the
long meeting in the forest which was bound to follow the
sky-shouting. Every one of the long-haired, dirty terrorists would speak at length, possibly for hours, for or
against sending anyone to the letter point. In this heated
debate the fact that the letter had been planted by a
party of unarmed men who did not conceal their tracks

could swing everything in our favour. Such details had
made or marred operations before.

But we soon regretted our lack of firepower when we
stumbled onto a large herd of elephant browsing in the
shade of the forest. No sooner had we come upon them,
than one particularly inquisitive young elephant ran
towards us. We stood and sweated—for this was the sort
of thing that could have brought the mother literally
down on top of us, but fortunately the little devil turned
round and made off back to the herd after circling once
round us.

When we eventually arrived at the Land Rover we
were shocked to find that our three guards had vanished.
They had discussed matters after our departure and
decided that the vehicle was too obvious a target for
Mau Mau. Fearing a concerted attack they had taken
refuge in a high tree some hundreds of yards further on.
So ended our trip to Mihuro. The first of our letters was
planted.

That night we slept in a friend's house at Nyeri, but
before dawn the next day were well on our way up the
mountain again on the way to Nyina wa Karathi. We
reached the slope after several hours' walking, to find
that three bull elephants were feeding just outside the old
Mau Mau food store where we wanted to place our letter.
All noiseless efforts to chase them away proved futile.
They just would not budge; so we sat down and waited
patiently for them to move on. But this they refused to do.
We sat looking at them—and our watches—until four
o'clock in the afternoon, then we had to leave if there
was to be any chance of getting back to the Land Rover
before darkness fell. Reluctantly we abandoned the pro-
ject and retraced our steps. It would have been far too
risky to plant the letter the next day. The sky-shouter
was going to be up at dawn, and we had no means of

contacting the pilot to postpone the flight. Ironically, six months and three days later, we captured a gang of terrorists led by a notorious Mau Mau leader named Ndungu Gicheru, who had, in compliance with the sky shout, spent two days looking for our non-existent letter at Nyina wa Karathi.

By the time we reached the vehicle we decided it was far too late to return to Nyeri, so we pushed out the spare wheel and slept in the back. By midnight the windows and canvas screens had a rough surface of frost on them, and the metalwork was so cold that it felt hot to touch. By two in the morning we could bear the cold no longer, so we jumped out and spent the rest of the night shivering on the leeward side.

The rock at the end of Wanderers' Track, the rock which Kimathi claimed he had put there, was only a matter of a few miles uphill from our frozen bivouac. As soon as the sun came over the horizon and we had thawed out, we drove on up to it, planted our letter with an empty bottle and stick, just as we had done at Mihuro. Then we set off down the mountain again, with Tony sitting on the bonnet photographing the game with his cine camera. The condition of some of the animals we encountered was pitiful. There were elephant and rhino with deep, long scars running along their bodies; there were others with crippled legs, and one or two with large gaping holes in their ears. Some colobus monkeys had had their beautiful long black and white hair singed or burnt. All this was the result of air bombardment and strafing, and, judging from the amount of wounded game we saw, the slaughter of animals must have been immense. What a tragedy that this beautiful mountain should have suffered from the destructiveness of man! Yet, on that lovely sunny day, with the wild flowers in bloom, and the crystal-clear streams dancing down the mountainside, it seemed as though nature was retaliating with beauty.

On the 23rd of December, three days later, we went back into the Aberdares to see whether either of our two letters had been removed. By this time the sky-shouter had completed its task. As before, the first point we visited was Mihuro, where we found that our letter had been destroyed by a school of Sykes monkeys, who had eaten all but a few fragments of the paper and thrown our empty bottle into the bush. We had to forge a new letter. Our early feeling of buoyant excitement had evaporated as we groped our way back to the Land Rover in silence.

The next day we visited the Rock. Here both our letter and bottle had gone, and for a moment we held our breath with excitement, but on looking behind the rock we were horrified to find a pile of empty corned beef tins. It was not the Mau Mau who had taken our message away, but a road-reconnaissance unit of the Royal Engineers, who thought they had found a treasure for the Intelligence, and had taken our letter, plus the bottle with our fingerprints on it, straight to the police in Nyeri. This was disastrous. The Rock was obviously a poor bet now, for even if we forged another letter and left it there, no Mau Mau would consider visiting the place once they had seen a group of hungry soldiers sitting there eating corned beef. The Rock thus joined Nyina wa Karathi in the list of failures, and left us with Mihuro, where our prospects were far from good. Losing two of the three letter points within the first three days was tragic. Christmas passed unhappily.

What could we do next? Early on Boxing Day morning Tony and I were sitting in Special Branch Headquarters when the telephone rang. On the far end of the line was Superintendent John Toft, at that time the

head of the Police Division at Naivasha. Beside the Forest
Station at North Kinangop, far down the western slope
of the Aberdares, a typical Mau Mau letter had been
found in a cleft stick early that morning. The letter was
addressed to 'Kinyanjui', my Kikuyu nickname. It was
written in Kikuyu and had not been translated for
security reasons. Without a moment's delay Tony and I
rushed to Naivasha to read the letter. The author, we
found, was a terrorist who had once held a fairly high
rank within the hierarchy of Mau Mau. His name was
Gati, and his letter read:

To Sar Kinyanjui of Special Branch.

If you find this letter please say so from an aeroplane.
I have heard the words so wait for me on the Nyeri
track and you will find another letter.

It is I, GATI.

That the letter should have been addressed to me was
not very surprising, for after the two series of expeditions
which I and other Special Branch officers had made into
the forests in 1954 and in 1955 to try to convince the Mau
Mau of the futility of violence, I had received an endless
stream of letters from the forest; some threatening, some
saying that isolated terrorists wished to surrender, some
saying almost nothing at all. 'I have heard the words.'
Obviously the writer had heard the sky-shout, which I
had recorded on tape in Kikuyu.

The following morning at dawn the Pembroke sky-
shouter was up again over the western Aberdares, confirming receipt of the letter, and saying that I would be
travelling along the Nyeri track on the 29th of December.
The weather over the mountain was stormy that day,
and the flight buffeted the pilot, who reported, on his
return, that he was doubtful if anyone could have heard
our message. But whether the message had been heard

or not, the die was cast for the 29th, and the date could not be changed.

From the place in which the letter was found it was obvious that by 'Nyeri track' the writer meant the Fort Jerusalem track which winds steeply up through the Aberdare forest from the timber mills at North Kinangop to the frost-worn Moorlands, then across the Moorlands towards Mihuro on the eastern side, before finally dropping down to Nyeri. There is no other track over the Aberdares from the west to Nyeri.

In dry weather the Fort Jerusalem track is bad enough and passable only if there have been no landslips, but in the rainy season, or after a heavy storm, no vehicle of any sort can get through. Gati could hardly have chosen a worse meeting-place. Having heard about the terrific storm from the pilot, we all looked forward to a great deal of walking. It was always necessary when travelling along this track in wet weather to get out and prop up one side of the vehicle, while the driver edged it across the slippery patches of ground where it was in particular danger of capsizing.

As we expected, the 29th was upon us before the forest had dried out. As we began climbing with the Land Rover strained in first gear, low ratio, we slithered about—buckling the wings of the vehicle time and time again against the banks, and showering everything, including ourselves, with mud. If the track was as bad as this on the slopes of the mountain, where the water could drain away, it would certainly be quite impassable when we reached the flatter, marshy Moorlands.

All the time we were looking for the promised letter. On and on we rumbled, only stopping when the windscreen was so covered with mud that we could not see through it. We had climbed to about 8,000 feet when we came upon the message. It was tied with forest string to a short bamboo stick standing upright in the middle of the track.

There it hung, and this was what admirers of Hemingway would call 'a moment of truth'. My thoughts skipped, grasshopper-style, but they always came back to one theme—that I was walking straight into an ambush, where every advantage of attack and retreat would lie with the terrorists. I probably wouldn't even know where the bullets had come from.

We stopped the Land Rover about thirty yards short, and sat quietly for a moment or two. No one could be seen. I got out and walked up to the bamboo stick. Once again we were all unarmed so as not to frighten anyone who might be watching us from the forest. But it was now too late to think about guns and protection. As I untied the string round the message and lifted it from the stick there was still no sound in the forest. I read it. It was a short message. All it said was, 'Return here again on January 1st.' This, oddly enough, was excellent news. Mau Mau do not normally put in an appearance when you first arrive at a meeting-place. They lie up in the forest nearby to see how you behave, whether you are armed, how many people come with you, and whether your pockets bulge, for that, in their eyes, is a sure sign that you are carrying grenades and planning to kill them. If they do in fact show themselves at the first meeting, you have every reason to suspect that something is wrong. On the other hand, any delay or hesitation on their part, any postponement of an arrangement to meet, is usually a sign that they really do want to meet you, but are frightened to come out before they have sized you up.

Knowing that we were being watched, I scribbled a reply saying we would be back there on the 1st, put it back in the cleft stick, lit a cigarette, and walked as casually as possible back to the Land Rover. We drove on up the track for some distance before we could find a place to turn round. On our way back we carefully edged our way round the stick to avoid knocking it over.

On New Year's Day we were back again. This time I brought with me my wife's Arab-silver bracelet which I had bought at Malindi on our honeymoon. Since the outbreak of the emergency I had taken it with me, tied firmly to a handkerchief, on most of my trips into the forest. I was confident that it would bring us luck again. It was our fetish.

Once again we stopped the Land Rover about thirty yards short of the bamboo stick, which was stuck in exactly the same place. Wedged in the cleft was a Government surrender pamphlet, on the back of which was written: 'Wait, we are here.' Whom would the next few minutes bring? For almost half an hour we walked up and down between the stick and the Land Rover. We smoked, we talked, we waited. No hands went into pockets, no one moved suddenly. No one stared into the forest. We were so keyed up that we found it difficult to keep still for more than a few seconds, and for want of something better to do, we drew lots to see who would be the first to be boiled in a Mau Mau tub.

Then we all heard a faint rustling in the forest to our left. Straining our ears we could hear the noise moving closer and closer. They were coming! We stopped talking, and our hearts began to beat faster. A feeling of expectancy is always pleasant, but when this expectancy is coupled with a little risk or anxiety it is even pleasanter. But still no one looked at the forest.

Seconds later two Mau Mau terrorists appeared about twenty yards away on the fringe of the forest. One was dressed in a reddish-brown bushbuck skin coat and an old, heavily patched pair of long, black trousers. The

KIKUYU WITCH DOCTOR   *Hulton Picture Library*

STUDYING AN OPPOSITE RIDGE IN THE TREE TOPS SALIENT
FOR RHINO BEFORE MOVING ON

A MEMBER OF ONE OF OUR TEAMS EMERGING FROM DEDAN
KIMATHI'S HIDE-OUT IN THE MIHURO AREA

other wore a monkey-skin jacket with soft hyrax skin trousers. Their hair was long and drooped over their faces. It was plaited, and the many plaits jutted out at all angles like the quills of a porcupine. (This plaiting of hair, incidentally, was a characteristic of all forest terrorists and was done so that they would find it easier to see and pick out the great numbers of lice which infested their heads.)

There on the fringe they paused to look at us, the one in the lead crouching down to peer through a thick bush. After studying us for a short while, both jumped quite boldly down onto the track and started towards us. I went forward to meet them and, as was customary, shook hands without saying a word. There was a silence for a minute or two as they turned to look suspiciously at the Land Rover, and then at my trouser pockets. Seemingly satisfied, one of them raised his arm and, pointing at the forest above, exclaimed:

'*Ndi o haria no ngumenyaga niwe Kinyanjui.*' ('Even from up there I knew you were Kinyanjui.')

'How?' I asked.

'Because I saw you in the Chinga forest in May during the talks,' he replied. This had been the last of the unsuccessful surrender conferences.

Feeling unexpectedly comforted by this news of our having met before, I told the man in the bushbuck coat, who was clearly the leader, and who was Gati, the letter writer, to fetch any other terrorists who might be waiting nearby. He assured me that they were alone. Both were carrying long double-edged 'simis' or Kikuyu swords which dangled from a strap over their shoulder, both smelt dreadfully—they had not washed for some months—but neither possessed a gun.

I beckoned them to sit down to talk, and after they had studied the Land Rover closely for a second time, we

c

moved over to a patch of grass and began what turned
out to be a three-hour conversation, throughout which,
as we spoke in their native tongue, they watched every
movement with extreme suspicion. Needless to say this
feeling was mutual, and our eyes kept as close a watch on
them as theirs did on us.

At first the conversation moved jerkily. For many
minutes we talked pointlessly about the state of the track
and the damage it had done to our Land Rover; about
Longonot and Eburru Hills, which we could see far
away down the mountain in the distance; about the
smell of petrol from the Land Rover which was so alien
to our two terrorists that it caused them to screw up their
faces in disgust and spit on the ground. All the time we
were weighing each other up. All the time we were
growing more used to each other. For this first conversation with Gati and his companion Hungu was not only
the end of the beginning of our scheme, but the beginning of the end of Dedan Kimathi. It was the key to the
ultimate success of our whole venture.

After some time I said I was going to have a cigarette,
and as they watched with renewed suspicion, I took out
a packet from my pocket. As a gesture of friendliness I
pulled two cigarettes out of the neatly packed rows,
placed them on the lid of the opened packet, and offered
them to our unusual companions. Instead of taking the
two cigarettes I had offered them, they dug their fingers
deep into the rows and pulled out a different two, obviously determined to avoid touching anything I had
chosen for them in case it contained some 'urogi' or
spell which would endanger them. But as time passed,
as we chatted on and the conversation ranged over a
score of irrelevant subjects, the first tension began to sub-
side, and in a more relaxed atmosphere their reason
for writing to me gradually emerged. Gati, at one time

the so-called Division General Quartermaster of the two-thousand-strong Mburu Ngebo Mau Mau army, told their story while Hungu periodically nodded in agreement.

It seemed that they had been checking their game snares on the Moorlands near Rurimeria hill on the 11th of December, when they had suddenly and unexpectedly come face to face with Kimathi and his powerful body-guard. Now Hungu had, long before, been Kimathi's prisoner, and had escaped while awaiting eighty strokes with a lash for the serious Mau Mau offence of having sexual intercourse with a female terrorist when he was not a privileged leader. For the even graver offence of escaping he knew he would be killed if caught again. When he saw Kimathi's men, therefore, he fled as he had never fled before.

Gati, on the other hand, had not known of Hungu's mistake until that moment. He was completely taken aback when he saw his companion run for dear life. But his mind worked fast. He knew that Kimathi believed in guilt by association. He knew that Kimathi would suspect them both of being pseudo-terrorists or spies for the Government, and that he would be strangled if he were caught. He realised that his only hope also lay in running away, and so he fled. Both men escaped from Kimathi's pack. By sheer luck they met again several hours later and several miles away.

They knew that Kimathi would try to hunt them down, as indeed he did, so our two fugitives had travelled on for two days and two nights until they located the powerful gang of another Mau Mau leader named Chege Karobia, from whom they sought protection. Chege agreed that they were not traitors, but he would not allow them to join his gang. He knew that if Kimathi heard of it, he would be blamed for not sending them

back for trial. And Kimathi was dangerous. He had
people strangled for far less than that!

Dispirited and frightened, Gati and Hungu left Chege
and went into hiding on their own. But as the days passed
their fear of Kimathi became an obsession. They became
too frightened to sleep; they imagined the ghastly consequences of being captured by Kimathi's men. They were
desperate, hunted by Mau Mau and the Security Forces
alike.

Then suddenly on the 20th of December they heard
the drone of an aeroplane over the Aberdares. The sound
came closer. In their own words, 'The aeroplane spoke.
It said we could write a letter. We knew it had been
sent by God to save us, so we wrote a letter and put it
beside the military camp below North Kinangop on
Christmas night when all the troops would be having a
party, and nobody would be out hunting us.'

'Why didn't you put your letter where the aeroplane
said?' I asked Gati.

'We did not hear any place mentioned, we only heard
the plane say we should write a letter.'

The stormy conditions on the Aberdares had distorted
the sky-shouter message to such an extent that only odd
words of it had been heard.

I asked Gati why he had addressed his letter to me,
and was told that 'as no other European speaks Kikuyu
from an aeroplane' he was sure it couldn't have been
anyone else. After hearing their story I asked the two of
them why exactly they had come to us that day.

'Before Kimathi kills us,' they said, 'we thought we
had better surrender.'

Tony and I summed up the situation. We had two
surrendered terrorists on our hands, and both had fallen
out of favour with Kimathi. On the other hand, not a
single person, apart from ourselves, knew they had sur-

rendered. In fact there was every likelihood of Kimathi hearing that they were not pseudo-terrorists when he next met Chege Karobia. After all, they would not have gone openly with their story to Chege if they had been traitors. Good use could be made of them, but we had to try to prove to the Mau Mau that they were still active in the forest. Otherwise their absence would compromise them and make them useless to us.

In the next few days we talked a lot to our two friends, until their fear of us had disappeared, and their outlook on life began to change. We showed them the reserves—so that they could see how Mau Mau had been eliminated. We took them up in helicopters. We told them what we knew about their own past activities in Mau Mau—so that they would appreciate that superior knowledge and might as well as right lay with us. Then we put them back into the Aberdare forest again and met them every few days to test their reliability. In the meantime we returned to Mihuro to see if our forged letter had been removed, but it had not.

All the time that Gati and Hungu were in the forest they were afraid that Kimathi would find them. To guard against this happening they kept very much to themselves, and avoided all the places where they knew other gangs had their hide-outs. We found them honest about their movements, and they were always punctual in their meetings with us. Soon we were completely satisfied with their trustworthiness, and issued them with pistols. This gave them a new confidence and they began to move more widely about the forest. All the time the task for which they were being prepared was developing behind the scenes.

Once we were certain that our guns were in safe hands we started making them popular with the other terrorists. We sky-shouted a message over several parts of the Aber-

dares claiming that both were badly wanted criminals
and offering £600 to anyone who gave information leading to their capture. We made a point of keeping Gati
and Hungu out of the forest when the sky-shouter broad-
cast this message, for they would have turned white at
the thought that we were encouraging people to run
them down. We did not keep this secret from them for
long, however, only long enough for us to get proof of
the reaction of the terrorists in the forest. The effect of
our hue and cry was dramatic. Within a few days Gati
and Hungu became heroes. Obviously they must have
committed some awful crime otherwise the Government
would not have put such a high price on their heads.
Everyone wanted to meet them. Not only had we boosted
their reputations to dazzling heights, but we had even
provoked Kimathi into changing his opinion about them.
He was now anxious to anoint them with fat, for they
were the only Mau Mau whose heads were worth as
much as was his own. We discovered this from the inter-
rogation of a terrorist named Gakoni who was wounded
and captured by a patrol of loyal Kikuyu guards while
stealing food in the reserve. He had been with his gang
leader when a letter had arrived from Kimathi calling
upon everyone to locate Gati and Hungu, for they had
done great deeds. This was just what we wanted. All was
well, provided that no one captured them and claimed
the reward!

To this day I think it was a miracle that out of all the
Mau Mau in the forest it should have been Gati and
Hungu who walked into our hands on that New Year's
Day. Throughout the first three years of the emergency
I had been in contact with many hundreds of Mau Mau.
I met and interrogated many who had surrendered. I
met captured terrorists shortly after they had come into
our hands. I met terrorists at the moment of their cap-

ture, and I met terrorists in their hide-outs during surrender talks. To me they were all alike—they all had the
same fanaticism, the same sullenness, the same suspi-
cions, and the same violent hate of anything not in tune
with their life inside the forest. Even those who surrendered because they could not stand the hardships of
forest life cherished warm memories of their semi-animal
life in the jungle. Over and above all this, they all seemed
to share the same fears and superstitions and to possess
an arrogance and a lust for killing which, for them, was
really an entertainment. I had not met one terrorist who,
at the moment of contact, did not justify this assessment
to a greater or lesser degree. But for the first time on that
New Year's Day I found an exception to this rule—Gati.
He was basically different from all those who had come
before him and from all those who came after him. He
was quite open about his life as a terrorist. He repented
but he asked for no mercy. He was incredibly polite and
soft-spoken. To tell a lie was, in his ears, a most terrible
thing. Above all else he was utterly fearless.

Gati had been a carpenter-handyman on a farm in
Kipipiri before the emergency, and had been sent back
to the reserve with the other Kikuyu labourers in the
area when the trouble began. But he had no roots in the
reserve and few friends. When the move to the forest
started there was little to hold him back, though he was
older than most of the recruits for the forest gangs.

Inside the forest his abilities were soon recognized. He
became the leader of a gang of two hundred, and as
quartermaster-general of an 'army' his special responsibility was stealing food from European farms. He had
been an efficient gang leader, but he was never a fanatic,
and did not, in fact, take any Mau Mau oaths until his
career as a leader was under way.

Towards the end of January we began to tell our two

friends from the mountain, as they liked to call themselves, about our plans for catching Kimathi. They were quite enthusiastic about it. We did not have to introduce them gradually to the idea that Kimathi was the root of all evil in the jungle. That had already become obvious to them.

Yet there was more to their readiness to help us than that. Gati and Hungu could see how the 'white enemy' they had been taught to hate had come to meet them unarmed and then given them guns with which to protect themselves. This contrast was so great, so traumatic, that they felt they now had to offer their lives to their old enemies. They realized that Kimathi had kept the Mau Mau in the forest by lies. They had been cheated, they thought. 'Ngai,' they insisted, 'had created a new magic. The forest would become a den of plague.'

The time was ripe for us to get together to discuss what our next step was going to be. How could Kimathi be eliminated? Hour after hour, day after day, we probed, and studied, and listened to everything Gati and Hungu had to say. They were now our most expert advisers, but it was clear that there was no easy road ahead for us. Kimathi was far too cunning to fall easily. Even if our two collaborators could merge with his gang without losing their lives, they would not be allowed to come face to face with him until they had first been screened, searched and questioned by his henchmen.

In the whole forest there were only two terrorists who were allowed to meet Kimathi without first being screened by his guards. They were Kahiu Itina, who led a gang some thirty strong in the northern Aberdares, and Chege Karobia, a close friend of Kimathi, who led a group of terrorists in the western Aberdares. Chege was the leader from whom our two men had sought refuge after their flight from Kimathi on the Moorlands.

We now knew for certain that we would have to have the support of members of Kimathi's own gang before we could account for him. It had to be an inside job, as no one else, apart from Kahiu Itina and Chege Karobia, had access to him. We were now faced with the question whether Kahiu and Chege or Kimathi's own bodyguard would be easiest to locate. Our two collaborators told us that it would be almost impossible to trace Kimathi's gang. You could search the jungle for months and never set eyes on them. By far the best course was to hunt for Kahiu Itina and Chege Karobia, both of whom would know where Kimathi was hiding and how best he could be dealt with. Once either one of them was in our hands, the jump to Kimathi would be a short one, or so we thought.

But even the task of locating Kahiu or Chege was not going to be an easy one. They too could be literally anywhere on the six thousand square miles of the Aberdares, and the fact that Gati and Hungu had met Chege after their flight from Kimathi on the Moorlands did not mean that they knew where he was and could go back and find him again.

We asked Gati what he thought about our letter scheme. Would Kimathi send any of his men to a letter point like Mihuro? He roared with laughter.

'Kinyanjui,' he said. 'That man is not a human being. If he heard of anything like that he would go many miles away. Even if you put thirty rifles there and told him he could have them, he would leave the area with great speed.'

This now showed us the futility of planting more letters, or of sky-shouting once again. We knew that all the elaborate plans we had made for the hunt for Kimathi were useless. We had not kept abreast with the times —Kimathi had changed a great deal since the days when

c*

the ex-terrorists we questioned had known him, since the days when he would have tried to murder anyone who wrote to him and invited him to surrender. Still, our scheme had not been entirely unproductive, for it had brought, somewhat indirectly, Gati and Hungu into our hands, and they had furnished us with the most up-to-date information about the changes that had taken place in the jungle.

On the 15th of February two terrorists were wounded and captured while trying to steal sheep from a farm in the country west of the Melawa river which flows down the north-western side of the Aberdares. On being questioned about Gati and Hungu they told us that as far as the people in the forest knew both our friends were still very active in the forest. One said that he had heard that Gati had murdered three policemen in Kiambu, and was now the subject of a hue and cry for £600! The other insisted that he had received a letter from Hungu only ten days before, saying he was in the Eland Hill area at the northern end of the Moorlands. This was all pure invention, of course, and one did not have to look far for a motive. Nevertheless, between the bluff and the lies there was an element of truth, and we were extremely pleased to know for certain that all was well in the forest for our two men.

Chapter Six

THE FORCE BUILDS UP

Murunguru utuhaga na ime

The bushcat skips in the dew

or

The early bird catches the worm.

OUR immediate aim now was the capture of either Kahiu Itina or Chege Karobia. Neither of our two men had any doubt that they would be able to merge with either of these gangs and speak to their leaders once they were able to find them, nor did they consider that either would deny them information about Kimathi once we had them in our hands. But how were we going to capture them?

'You will know we are dead when you find your pistols in years to come,' said Gati.

We realized all too well that our two friends could do very little alone against such powerful opponents.

From that moment we set out to build up our force, which we aimed to do by joining, and then capturing, small Mau Mau gangs. Meanwhile we decided to avoid Kahiu Itina and Chege Karobia, and Kimathi as well, until we had a minimum of twelve hard-core terrorists on our side. Twelve, we estimated, would be adequate for our purposes, provided that they carried sufficient fire-power.

Our first move in this new direction began on the 28th of January 1956, exactly four weeks from the day

75

when Gati and Hungu came into our hands. Before dawn Tony, Gethieya and I were making our way up a narrow game track in the Melawa Gorge. As only a terrorist could guide us in the darkness—for they could see surprisingly well at night—Gati was in the lead. We were worried about being trailed and identified by some Mau Mau foraging gang returning to the forest after a raid into the wheatlands below, so as we travelled along Hungu was in the rear threading back the blades of grass every few yards to mislead anyone who might try to follow. Our faces and arms were blackened, and we wore the customary terrorist uniform of animal skins. We had specially-made wigs of terrorist hair, but these fitted so firmly over our heads and made us sweat so much that, in the darkness, we pulled them off and carried them along in our hands, just as a Red Indian would carry the scalp of his victim.

Gati was going to take us to a secret path in the forest often used by terrorists crossing the Melawa Gorge. There, by the path, Tony and I were going to wait, ready to intercept anyone who came along, while Gati and Hungu went on to comb the forest south of the river. Some weeks before they had left two small gangs there searching for a suitable place to build an underground food store. Our two friends were confident that the gangs would still be in the area, as much grain was ready for reaping on the European farms in the valley below, and this was a powerful attraction to hungry terrorists. Then again no terrorists would think of constructing something fairly permanent like a food store if they were not planning to stay. Our friends were sure that, if any of the terrorists did succeed in getting away, they would run right into our ambush.

As we got near the edge of the Moorlands, the first glimmer of dawn was appearing in the east, and we hurried across the open grassland as fast as we could to try and reach the thick forest before there was enough light to show us up. We were wet through from the dew and the frost on the grass, but we were still sweating. The secret path was barely visible in the half-light when we reached it. It ran through thick deciduous forest where falling leaves had given the ground a soft mulchy layer. It was a natural escape route for a fugitive—dark and thickly hemmed in, reasonably flat to allow for speed, noiseless to tread on, while the continuous shower of leaves falling from the trees would soon hide any terrorist tracks.

While Gati and his companion set off down the hillside on their own, Tony, Gethieya and I checked our Patchett guns and lay down in ambush positions beside the track. The day passed slowly without incident, though we were bitten mercilessly by ants. Several times we heard a rustling of the bushes nearby, but each time it turned out to be some little forest animal scampering about in search of food or on its way to water. Once a beautiful little red forest duiker came along the track and passed us unsuspectingly. The first feeling of excitement began to wear off, and by evening we were all beginning to get cramped and restive. As the sun fell away behind the horizon teams of Colobus monkeys sounded their good-nights in the low, rolling, guttural call which echoes eerily for miles round the forest. When the Colobus had retired in silence, the birds became quiet, and to mark the end of day came the excited cackle of the partridges who always seem to leave their homecomings till too late.

Suddenly, as we lay in silence, there was a low whistle, followed a few seconds later by another. For a moment I wondered whether it was a terrorist signal, and I clutched my gun more tightly. Then we heard it again, this time it was a little louder, and I thought that it must be Gati,

who knew where we were lying. He was probably
frightened to walk towards us in case we should make a
mistake and shoot him. I whistled back and then listened
again. This time my whistle was answered by two short,
sharp whistles. Yes, it was Gati all right.

His dark, stocky form soon appeared. He was alone.
Without a moment's hesitation he walked over to where
I was lying just as though he could see me from a distance and, bending down, put out his hand for me to
shake. I could feel immediately that his wrist and fingers
were covered with congealed blood.

'*Kai niatia?*' ('What is it, Gati?') I asked. 'Where is
Hungu?'

'There is nothing bad. They are sitting back there,
and Hungu is guarding them,' he replied, pointing down
the path. I breathed a sigh of relief.

In no time Gati was leading us back through the pitch-
dark forest and within a hundred yards we came upon
Hungu. He was standing, feet apart, pistol in hand, over
the prone bodies of four Mau Mau who were handcuffed
in pairs and lying face downwards on the ground.

It seemed that shortly after our two collaborators had
left us early that morning they came to the banks of the
Melawa river. They had followed the river downstream
for nearly three miles before they found a place where
fragments of plucked leaves were lying on the bank. Mau
Mau often used these to cover the river stones and thus
avoid leaving muddy marks on them when drawing
water from the middle of the stream. From that point
they had tracked the gang through the forest for a long
way. They had seen where the gang had rested, where
one terrorist had branched off to examine a hollow in a
tree for honey, and where, eventually, the gang had
taken extreme precautions to cover their own tracks.
This was one of the arts which the remaining hard-core

terrorists had perfected. It involved putting the whole weight of the body on to one side of the foot so that no toe or heel marks would be noticeable. When they ran through long grass a thin stick would be used to thread the blades back every few paces. Once a gang began covering its tracks, a technique which Mau Mau referred to with justifiable pride as 'kuhitha makinya', or 'to hide the feet', only the most expert jungleman could follow them, and that, in my experience, only meant Mau Mau of the same calibre as the hunted.

Suspecting, because of these precautions, that the hideout was near, Gati and Hungu waited until the mists thickened in the valley, for they knew that only then would the gang light a fire. When the mist was thick and swirling, they quietly moved downwind in the hope of smelling the smoke. And that was exactly what directed them to the hideout.

Our friends crept up on their hands and knees to within ten yards of a gang of five terrorists. Two were asleep on the ground, a third was sitting with his head resting on his knees, and the two others were preparing to cook some buck meat over the smoking fire. The attack was launched so quickly that all the terrorists had been able to say was, '*Noguo, noguo.*' ('That's it, that's it.') But while Hungu was busy handcuffing them, one had jumped to his feet and tried to escape through the dense forest. Gati fired at him. Two shots went astray, but the third bullet cut into his thigh and knocked him over. For a moment he lay there, then he rose again and plunged through some bushes, but a few seconds later another shot hit him in the back of the neck, killing him instantaneously. Gati searched him quickly for arms and documents, getting blood all over his hands. Then he led the party round in a long detour to our rendezvous. The journey was uphill all the way and took most of the day.

After Gati's return we moved on immediately, without waiting for the dawn, as the open Moorlands had to be crossed again, and we wanted to be out of sight of terrorist eyes by dawn. As we trekked back nobody said a word until one of the prisoners turned to Hungu and asked him to remove the handcuffs, as they would have no hope of escape if a wild animal were to charge while they were manacled together.

'I did not harvest you to plant me,' Hungu retorted, and the journey continued with only the soft thud of our feet breaking the quietness of the night.

The newcomers were brought all the way back to Nairobi, where we set up a base-camp called 'Mayfield'. There we began the tedious task of winning their support and confidence. Like all Mau Mau from the heart of the forest, they were astonished by the ordered flow of life outside, where there was now little evidence of an emergency. They knew of the damage that terrorism had wrought in their tribal reserve. Now they could see the spectacular progress made by Government in its efforts to rehabilitate the Kikuyu.

By showing them the peaceful conditions in the reserve, we shattered to smithereens their ridiculous notion that the Mau Mau would win. We then embarked upon a deflating campaign designed to convince them that they were not the tough, superhuman fighters they thought they were. We took them to a rifle range and showed them what poor marksmen they were. We took them up in a helicopter where, by cutting the engine and dropping fast, we made them decidedly anxious to get their feet onto solid ground again.

When their arrogance had vanished, education began. There were endless hours of patient discussion in which the futility of terrorism and the malevolence of their leaders had to be emphasized and re-emphasized. We explained how the leaders had perverted the tribal rituals and oaths, we explained why and how the leaders were debauching the rank and file. We explained the appalling suffering which Mau Mau had brought upon the tribe, and the effect of this upon the young children who had been made parentless by Mau Mau violence. The methods of conversion were many, but the key to their success was kind and gentle handling. Our prisoners fed well, and they were treated well. Another vital factor was, of course, the presence of Gati and Hungu, who, as Mau Mau themselves, were able to argue with greater effect than any white man. But of all the many factors to which their conversion can be attributed, the most telling was the freedom they were given from the moment they were brought out of the forest. While they were watched discreetly by Gati, Hungu and ourselves, they were never impounded as prisoners. They retained the weapons they had carried in the forest and were free to roam about our camp with them. This was a risky business, but it was the only means of testing their loyalty and we always felt it was better to establish this, as far as one could, while outside the forest, and before we placed ourselves at their mercy inside it.

It was not very long before they were sufficiently indoctrinated for our purpose; in nine or ten days we saw a marked difference. But on no account would we ever let them wash or change their forest clothes, as it was important that physically they should remain in the same state as they were when captured.

By the end of the first week in February we were confident that we had six collaborators, and back to the Aberdares we went. Meanwhile, one of the newcomers had told us about a Mau Mau meeting scheduled to take place on the 8th of February beside a stream called the Magomboki. As a result our six terrorists were put into the Kipipiri forest on the night of the 7th with orders to attend the meeting. We did not want them to capture anyone, but we hoped their attendance would prove that they were still in circulation, and that this would pave the way for subsequent operations.

It rained heavily on the 8th, and we wondered how much this would hamper the conference. The four new boys roamed about the Magomboki stream all day, but nobody put in an appearance. Gati and Hungu, tired of sitting in the rain, cut through the forest to a large timber mill known as Bush Mills, which had been burnt to the ground by Mau Mau early in the emergency, and came upon the tracks of two terrorists who seemed to have gone up and down one path several times that day. They decided to wait and see whether anyone passed by again. Patience was soon rewarded. Some three hours later two Mau Mau carrying large bundles of wheat on their backs, came climbing up through the forest. They did not see their ambushers slip round behind them, and both were pulled to the ground from behind so suddenly that the straps of their bundles, which were fastened round their necks, almost strangled them. When they realized what had happened they were furious, and accused Gati and Hungu of trying to steal the food they had taken such grave risks to obtain. However, when they saw our men draw their pistols they quickly stopped arguing and were brought back to us in a very worried state.

In those days no Mau Mau gang moved far from its own chosen area, but the gangs knew their own homeland in great detail. Our own pseudo-operations had caused this immobility. Meanwhile, while we were trying to find out which part of the forest was Dedan Kimathi's select area, we thought it essential to raise our force from as many places as possible in order to gain a wide knowledge of the terrain all over the Aberdares.

Our two latest additions were indoctrinated somewhat more quickly than the others because this time, as
on all future occasions, we were able to use a larger
number of their own kind on the job. Within a few days
we found we were able to spring our eight-strong force
onto another part of the mountain, the Fort Hall forest.
At this time of the year, hot and sunny before the seasonal long rains, the forest is a picture of natural magnificence, with the trees and bushes in full flower and the
bees humming from plant to plant in a constant search
for pollen. As honey was one of the staple foods of the
terrorists, it was a normal practice for gangs to send out
small scouting parties to pinpoint beehives so that when
the rains eventually did come they could find the honey
easily. This search for hives inevitably meant a considerable increase in gang movement, and because of this
we were a little concerned about the safety of our
men. There was always the possibility that they would
run into Kimathi's gang and be captured, for it was his
practice to hold and interrogate every terrorist he came
across. Some way of supporting our team while it was
operating had to be found. We therefore decided that
Tony, Gethieya and I would set up a base in the forest
to which, if events turned out badly, our team could run,
or from which, if we heard firing, we could rush out.

The base we established for this operation in the Fort
Hall forest consisted of a small canvas bivouac, hardly
larger than a bed sheet, sited on the southern bank of a
river called the Mathioya where the forest was sufficiently dense to keep us completely concealed. As the
team began a search of the forest, we took up our positions.

We had been in our tiny camp for only an hour or so
when we realized that the firing of pistols would serve no
practical purpose as a warning signal by day. The gases

trapped between the intersecting links of bamboo expanded in the hot sun and split the poles in an endless volley of loud explosions which echoed all round the forest. It was quite impossible to distinguish between these explosions and gunfire. Nevertheless, we took it in turn to sleep and someone was on the alert at all times.

Meanwhile our team was moving silently through the undergrowth studying the movement of the bees, seeing if the Mau Mau had visited new hives, searching for tracks, for game snares, for watering-points and for other telltale signs of terrorist activity. They discovered there was ample food for Mau Mau in the area, as duiker and bushbuck were plentiful and there was an unusually large variety of indigenous trees whose fruits were edible. There was also a great deal of thabai, that dreadful nettle which brings out a massive rash on your body, but which was a favourite Mau Mau foodstuff.

They stopped to examine each fruit-bearing tree and each patch of stinging nettle they came across. They carefully bent the nettles over with a stick to see whether any leaves had been plucked from the lower primaries. They knew the Mau Mau would never remove any of the upper leaves and thus reveal their visit. The first night came, and to avoid lighting a fire our team ate corned beef and buried the tins. They slept as a buck would sleep, where the ground was soft with their lair adequately hidden. It made no difference to them that the soil was moist and the dew dripped down on them from the leaves of the trees above.

By first light they were on the move again, snaking their way through the forest, hoping all the time to sniff a whiff of smoke from Mau Mau fires. They had not gone very far before they came to a slight rise in the ground. Here they halted to peer through the trees at the higher ground in front of them. As they were doing

this they heard a rustle in the forest close behind them.
They were being tracked down! But before they had
time to decide what to do, four terrorists came into view
and stopped abruptly twenty yards away. For a moment
both parties stood glaring at one another without moving
an inch or making a sound. Suddenly there was a shout
from Gati.

'*Urai*,' ('Run,') he called, and our men swung round
sharply and scattered into the forest.

'*Tigai kuura, no ithui*,' ('Don't run, it is only us,') the
terrorists yelled back as they chased after our men.

But our men were not running away from fright. They
had already identified the newcomers. There was Rukwaro, a Fort Hall man; Thia, a minute little fellow whose
size had made him the butt of many forest jokes; Wamai,
who was an expert at constructing home-made weapons,
and Kinuthia, a tall, thin terrorist who had once operated
far away on Mount Kenya. They were not dangerous like
Kimathi or Kahiu Itina or Chege Karobia. Gati had
shouted to his men to run only because he knew that if
his team had stood their ground the other band would
have fled instead. Running away from one another was
an accepted habit when two gangs met.

Convinced that our team was a genuine, friendly gang,
the four Mau Mau raced on through the forest appealing
to them to stop. When our men had run a few hundred
yards, Gati deliberately slowed them down so as to let
his pursuers catch up, and soon everyone was gathered
together in an excited, breathless group.

'*Kai*,' exclaimed the panting Rukwaro, 'we nearly
missed one another.'

'*Noguo*,' agreed Gati. 'That's it, we had gone like
arrows!'

At this everyone burst out laughing. In their excitement they did not care whether their enemies heard

them. There was much shaking of hands the terrorist way
—each clasp followed by much holding of thumbs before
clasping hands a second time. It was a happy reunion
among friends of the jungle.

By the time the team and their four new prisoners
arrived at our forest base, the newcomers had been told
all about our scheme, and were already quite pleased at
the idea of joining us, especially as Gati and the others
seemed to be so happy in their work. But they were
frightened of meeting a European. They had, after all,
only caught fleeting glimpses of them during the forest
operations of the past three years. My first impression of
them was their nauseating smell. It was so strong that I
found I could not stand near them. The feeling was evi-
dently mutual, for one of them instantly vomited on
smelling a bar of soap taken from Gethieya's pocket. In
the days to come I saw many terrorists sickened by the
smell of soap on our bodies. Nothing seemed to revolt
them more than cleanliness.

The target of twelve which we had set ourselves before
we were prepared to turn our attention to Kahiu Itina
and Chege Karobia had now been reached. It had taken
us seven weeks to arrive at this stage. We were at last
ready to begin our search for the only two terrorists in
the forest, apart from Kimathi's own men, who could
lead us to Kimathi himself.

Chapter Seven

THE MEETING ON KIPIPIRI

Muti uguagira mundu uri ho

The tree falls on the man who stands by it

or

Trouble comes when we least expect it.

TEN days later we went back into the Kipipiri forest. Our terrorists were now in two teams of six, one under the leadership of Gati, the other under Hungu.

It was almost nine months to the day since the last surrender talks in the Chinga forest had broken down, and we knew that a migration of terrorists had taken place away from our old meeting-place in the eastern Aberdares towards Kipipiri and the northern part of the mountain. With that migration, we now discovered, went Kahiu Itina. He had once been a leading member of the Ituma Demi Trinity Council, a body set up in the forest by Kimathi in 1953 to direct the activities of the nine separate wings of the Ituma Demi Mau Mau army. We went north into the Kipipiri in search of him.

On the 24th of February each of the two teams picked up tracks in the forest, but by nightfall they had made no contact. The next day they continued the hunt, and by noon had converged on an empty Mau Mau hide-out close to the rocky summit of Kipipiri.

Kipipiri is surrounded by thick forest and bamboo which rises almost three-quarters of the way up her slopes. Above this there is a stretch of grassland, like the

Moorlands of the Aberdares in many ways, and above that again is the rocky summit. While our teams climbed they were both being carefully watched by a Mau Mau gang, and they had only just arrived at the hide-out when they heard voices calling from a ridge several hundred feet to their left. The callers had identified Gati and certain of our men, and were asking them to wait until they could come across the valley and join them.

To Gati's surprise, the other gang numbered no less than twelve. They carried four automatic weapons, and were led by a particularly well-known terrorist named Gaichuhie. The last time Gati had seen Gaichuhie was in August 1954, when he had been chosen by Kimathi as one of four so-called 'athuri' or elders to preside over the trial of a young terrorist named Gathongo. Gathongo had been seated one night with Gati and some thirty other terrorists round a fire in the Fort Hall forest when Kimathi had arrived on one of his inspections. All had gone well until the late hours of the night when, suddenly, three rounds of ammunition exploded in the fire. Everyone scattered in alarm. When the panic was over and everyone had regathered, Kimathi and his escort began a thorough investigation. He was sure that the ammunition had been thrown onto the fire deliberately to try and kill him, although everyone else was satisfied there had been an accident. Suspicion fell upon Gathongo, who, according to one of Kimathi's men, had seven rounds of ammunition in his pocket before the explosion, but only four afterwards. Gati, however, knew Gathongo had not been responsible because he had been sitting next to him all the time. Angered by the false accusations made by Kimathi's man, Gati strongly defended Gathongo and said he would not allow him to be strangled. This stand could have put Gati himself in danger, but he held a loaded sub-machine gun in his hands, and nobody, not even Kimathi, felt inclined to argue too much that night.

The next morning the argument began afresh, and it was obvious that if it weren't for Gati, Gathongo would have been strangled on the spot. News of the case spread quickly through the forest, and within days hundreds of Mau Mau were arguing about it. Some of them wanted to see Gathongo killed as a warning to any others who might be planning to attack Kimathi. Those who took this view were not in the least concerned about the strength of the evidence against Gathongo. All they wanted to see was someone die, and Gathongo was as good a victim as anyone else. Many terrorists, however, sided with Gati and said that nobody should be strangled unless there was proof of responsibility. The argument reached such a pitch that it was touch and go whether the two opposing camps would begin fighting among themselves. At this stage Kimathi chose four elders to settle the row, and Gaichuhie was one of them. Unlike the other three judges, who sought to ingratiate themselves with Kimathi by recommending Gathongo's execution, Gaichuhie would not agree to the strangulation without good reason. His stubbornness made him very unpopular, and he was threatened himself, but he literally stood by his guns and challenged all who accused him to a duel. In the end his personal courage and toughness, for he was a tough nut by any standard, won the day, and Gathongo was spared. Gati and Gaichuhie had parted as great friends after this incident and were delighted to meet again on Mount Kipipiri.

After exchanging excited greetings and smearing animal fat on the foreheads of our men in accordance with Mau Mau custom, both groups faced Mount Kenya, the home of their god Ngai, and, with arms upraised, said their prayers. The ritual was peculiar. As the traditional

god of the Kikuyu, Ngai, lived on the snow-capped peak
of Mount Kenya, and the Mau Mau believed that their
prayers would only be heard if they faced that mountain
as their forefathers had done years ago. They all stood together in close formation, earth in their right hands and
arms raised shoulder high. After some time Gati and Gaichuhie walked round together to the head of the group, a
position they were entitled to occupy as leaders, and
there, in turn, they began to speak. The words did not
follow any set form. They came out spontaneously.

'Ngai,' said Gaichuhie, 'you have chosen me as one to
lead your people. You have given us this forest to hide in,
the rivers to drink from, the berries to eat and the animal
skins to clothe ourselves in. You have told us to suffer so
that the nine clans of the Kikuyu can be cleansed of all
traitors and you have chosen a large red book in which
the names of all of us who die will be written, for they
will be more precious than those who remain alive.'

As Gaichuhie paused at the end of this and every
subsequent sentence, the Mau Mau behind him mumbled
their chorus.

'*Thaai, Thaaiya, Thaai, Haaaah!*'

This was a mark of agreement with what their leader
had said, and as they mumbled these words they released
some of the earth in their hands and allowed it to trickle
down to the ground. This, they believed, meant that
their prayers had been 'planted as a seed in the ground
and would therefore germinate' and be answered. When
Gaichuhie finished, Gati's turn came, and he prayed in
similar vein, his words too being planted with earth from
the hands of his motionless listeners. His words drew an
approving mumble '*Thaai, Thaaiya, Thaai, Haaaah!*' Even
to the Mau Mau the ceremony was a little frightening.

When the prayers were finished and they started talking to one another again, Gaichuhie said that there

were a great many terrorists over the crest of the mountain, possibly eight or ten gangs. Even more were expected to come that day because a big meeting had been called by a Mau Mau witch-doctor named Muraya, who would be arriving the following day with important news. Gati asked whether Kahiu Itina would be present, but all Gaichuhie would say was, 'Only Ngai knows that.' Gati did not pursue the question. A man who is inquisitive is a spy, and spies are strangled.

That night our teams slept with Gaichuhie's gang and did their fair share of sentry duty, well knowing that no Security Forces were in the forest as it had been closed to all troops. At first light the whole group moved over to the other side of the mountain. Here they found no less than eighty-two terrorists, at least half of whom were well known to our collaborators. Witch-doctor Muraya had not yet arrived, nor was there any sign of Kahiu Itina. All the Mau Mau were split up into groups of six or seven and were lying about on the rocks and grass within shouting distance of each other. Outside the main group there were several groups of armed sentries, posted in pairs. Beyond them, right at the top of the mountain, were several more sentries, all absolutely motionless with their backs against rocks.

As soon as they arrived, our men were given a warm welcome, for many had not seen them for several weeks, and no one had seen Gati or Hungu since our £600 had been put on their heads. Gati found his influence was so great that he was able to issue orders and organize the relief of sentries. As he wandered about among the terrorists, he recorded their names in a dairy farmer's milk ledger which he had confiscated from a colleague.

By three o'clock in the afternoon everyone was beginning to fidget. Witch-doctor Muraya had still not turned up, and everyone had been without food for almost twenty-four hours. To cook they had first to find water and this could only be done during daylight. By four o'clock it was unanimously agreed that if Muraya had not arrived within an hour, the meeting would be called off and everyone would go his way.

After all this time the terrorists had run out of conversation, and in boredom they stretched out on the grass and began to doze. Suddenly the silence was shattered by a shot. The gangs jumped to their feet and rushed for cover with their guns and knives at the ready. Hungu had fired the shot, and after the first moments of confusion his neighbours grabbed him, threw him to the ground, and seized his pistol. Had he tried to murder someone? Was he a traitor?

Within a minute, twenty to thirty terrorists were packed tightly round Hungu's prostrate body, questioning him sharply, and more were running over towards him. Our men knew that to speak out in favour of a suspected person was to court an unpleasant form of death, so they made no move. This was one of those occasions when matters had to be left to take their course. It was now up to Hungu whether Gati and all the rest of our men were to live or die. If our men ran they would certainly not get away from the mob, and they did not have enough guns to shoot their way out. All they could do was to wait and hope and pray as they had never prayed before.

Gati could hear Hungu answering the questions which were showered upon him so fast that he seldom had time to reply to one before three or four more were fired at him. He could hear Hungu's nervous voice stuttering and hesitating, but always just managing to get an answer out. So far he was holding his own. Then Gati heard a demand that Hungu be given a traditional test to make him speak the truth. This involved placing red-hot coals on his bare stomach and cutting off his thumbs at the first joint. Gati knew Hungu well enough to realize that he would never be able to withstand that torture. 'This is the day of our judgment,' Gati whispered to himself.

Then Gati could bear the strain no longer. He got up and walked over to the hostile mob which was getting increasingly hysterical. He elbowed his way through them as though he too were angry. After all, he was a popular leader—thanks to us. When he reached the middle, and was standing beside Hungu's feet, he raised his hand high above his head. Speaking in a firm authoritative voice, he ordered everyone to stand back and be silent. Gaichuhie in his usual stubborn way refused to obey.

'You, Gati,' he said. 'You were with Hungu. This is not an affair for you. Probably you are a spy too.'

All eyes turned on Gati. This was a moment for strength. He knew that what he was now going to say might provoke Gaichuhie to challenge him to a duel with knives, and one or the other, or both, would surely die a painful death. He knew that was the sort of thing which appealed to Gaichuhie's tough temperament. He had not forgotten Gathongo's trial in the forests of Fort Hall. But it was better to die fighting a duel with Gaichuhie than to be pulled to bits by a howling mob.

Gati lifted his hand and placed a finger on the bridge of his nose between his eyes.

'Look at me right here,' he said to Gaichuhie. 'And don't look anywhere else until I have finished.'

He could sense that the mob was already impressed with his strong words. They became silent and watched with startled eyes. Gati gave Gaichuhie a cold, steady stare, not daring to blink or glance away.

'Tell everyone here if we did not sleep with you last night! Tell them that while you and your men were asleep my men guarded you! Tell them, for you seem very full of words.'

There was a deathly silence as the mob awaited Gaichuhie's answer. Those harsh words were not likely to draw a soft reply from a tenacious, brutal tough like Gaichuhie. But no reply came; and, as the crowd began to stir and whisper, Gaichuhie shook his head, turned about and walked meekly away, leaving Gati in command of the situation. The crisis had passed, but all was not yet well. Gati turned to Hungu, and in the same firm voice asked him who he had fired at.

'*Aca*,' ('No,') replied Hungu. 'The gun fired by itself. It was in my pocket.'

'Give me his trousers,' ordered Gati, hoping and praying that what Hungu had said was true, for he was now going to point out the bullet-hole in the pocket. It was true. Gati held up the trousers so that everyone round him could see the hole, then, when they had done so, he threw the trousers on the ground beside Hungu and told him to put them on. The mob did not object. Some had already lost interest in the incident and were drifting away. Then he called for Hungu's skin jacket and the pistol and he was given these too. As with the trousers, he threw them down onto the ground and Hungu nervously took them. For the last time he raised his voice and said:

'All must leave here now. The shot will have been heard by our enemies.' And with that the mob dispersed. Many jeered at Gaichuhie, and some even said that he should be strangled for falsely accusing Gati.

A few minutes later only two terrorists, apart from those in our teams, were left at the meeting-place, but these two did not wish to leave by themselves. They had been living alone for many months after the gang to which they had belonged was broken up by the Security Forces. Three of their companions had been killed in the action and they were the only survivors. Both were natives of Iyego location of the Fort Hall district and when they saw that one of our men was also a native of Iyego, whom they had known since childhood, they decided they would try and join Gati's gang. The sight of this old friend was too much for them. They just could not leave him. And so the two had come up to Gati and asked permission to join his party. Naturally Gati was delighted and willingly agreed to their request. Out of a situation which seemed at one stage bound to end in catastrophe much good had come. For not only had Gati's leadership been confirmed, but our whole force had had its morale lifted and our strength had been increased by two.

Nevertheless, this incident on Kipipiri taught us an important lesson which we never forgot. If we had gone with our teams on the operation we would have compromised every single man. No retreat would have been possible over the open grassland, and no disguise, however good, would have enabled us, as Europeans, to mingle with the mob at the meeting-place. From that moment we resolved never to lead our teams in person unless the operation was one based on such good information that we could go straight to a target and attack it. When there was any searching through the forest to be done, or when there was a need to merge quietly with other Mau Mau gangs, we would leave things to our teams and restrict our own activities to ambushing key points, providing support, checking Mau Mau letter boxes, and contacting our teams at pre-arranged rendezvous in the forest. Having gone to all this trouble to establish a friendly Mau Mau gang in the Aberdares, no risk which might betray them was justified.

Although trouble had come to us when we least expected it, or, as the Kikuyu idiom says, 'The tree beneath which we were resting had nearly fallen on top of us,' the Kipipiri episode paved the way for operations against Kahiu Itina and other terrorist leaders. Our small but valuable force had been displayed before terrorists from many widely-scattered areas of the Aberdares and, with their return to their various haunts, went the knowledge that every one of our men was still active and friendly. This news circulated still further afield much to our advantage. Furthermore, it had been established that our target, Kahiu Itina, was nowhere near Mount Kipipiri or the western Aberdares, or he would certainly have been present at the meeting. We now turned our attention to the Wuthering Heights region of the northern Aberdares, which had been Kahiu's stamping ground in earlier days.

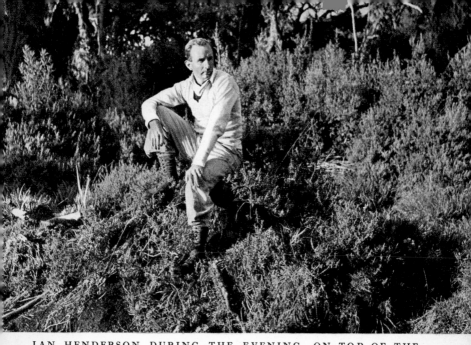

IAN HENDERSON DURING THE EVENING, ON TOP OF THE
ABERDARES

POLICE LAND ROVER FORCING A COURSE THROUGH THE
VEGETATION COVERING THE 'ELEPHANT JEEP TRACK' IN
THE TREE TOPS SALIENT

CHECKING ONE OF
DEDAN KIMATHI'S
'POSTS' OR
'LETTER BOXES'
IN THE
MWATHE REGION

HOW WE 'PLANTED'
OUR LETTERS TO
THE TERRORISTS
IN THE FOREST
AT THE BEGINNING
OF THE OPERATION

Chapter Eight

WITCH-DOCTOR KINGORI

Gwota mwaki ni kuhuria

To get the warmth of the fire
one must stir its embers

or

No gains without pains.

THROUGHOUT the month of March we operated at full
pressure in a determined bid to find Kahiu Itina before
the long rains broke. The teams made three contacts
with small Mau Mau gangs. We captured four more
terrorists and killed a further two, but we met no one who
had seen or heard of Kahiu Itina for many months.
These were small engagements but even so they contained
an element of danger. One incident was typical of the others.

Thirteen sheep had been stolen from a farm near
Naromoru, and the tracks of the animals were followed
by the police to the edge of the Aberdare forest. At their
request we put one of our teams into the forest to pick up
the spoor and track down the gang. Although the gang
had shown much skill in driving the sheep along well-
used game paths where the spoor of the game and sheep
merged, to the detriment of quick tracking, the team
eventually managed to find the place several miles up
the mountain where the animals had been slaughtered.

Much of the meat had been abandoned at this point,
which showed that the gang had been prepared to make
do with what they could carry, and to move on before

any soldiers or pseudos could come up on them. It looked, however, as though the gang was reasonably large, and we were hopeful that Kahiu Itina was responsible.

After filling their skin bags with some of the abandoned meat, our team continued the pursuit westwards over the rising ground towards Muir's Massif, which they reached at dusk. It was now too dark for them to see the tracks of the gang so they decided to rest until daybreak. The cold, howling winds of the upper Aberdares had dropped in the calm of the late evening, and our team lay back on the grass gazing down towards the Lol Daiga hills which were faintly visible more than fifty miles away, talking in subdued voices about the visits they had made to that far country to steal Nderobo cattle. As they were lying there, Njeru, the leader, suddenly heard an unfamiliar noise. He touched one of his talkative companions on the shoulder and then turned his head to one side to listen. A long way down below, in a thickly wooded ravine, a dry branch had cracked and fallen heavily to the ground. Seconds passed, then they all heard something. *Ka, ka, ka,* then a pause, *ka, ka.* Now they knew what it was. Someone was hacking at a tree. It was not the deep, heavy sound of the sort of axe used by forestry workers, but the finer and sharper noise which only a Mau Mau simi would make. It could only be Mau Mau at this time of the evening, Mau Mau looking for firewood to warm themselves during the night.

'If they are collecting firewood the *mbuchi* [hide-out] must be near,' said Njeru and, as one, the team rose, threw the straps of their skin bags over their heads, ruffled the grass where they had been lying, and hurried off round Muir's Massif and down the side of the mountain.

Soon they were on the edge of a deep ravine waiting

quietly for darkness to fall. They had hoped to hear terrorist voices from here, but the noise of the river below drowned all other sounds. When darkness came they moved cautiously through the brushwood, and had only gone a short way when they saw the flames of a fire flickering below them almost halfway up the far side of the ravine. They moved on slowly until they were only forty yards from the fire. Three terrorists were sitting round it. Each was holding a stick on which large pieces of meat were stuck and the meat was sizzling in the fire.

Our men reckoned that only three terrorists could not have carried all that meat by themselves, and that there must be others in the vicinity, so they decided to lie quietly until the meal was over and the three terrorists had gone to sleep. Then they would creep up and take the three by surprise. A half-moon was high in the sky before all was quiet round the fire. The three terrorists had not been joined by any others. They had eaten well, too well to do anything but sleep. They sat round the fire and talked for hours. At last they all stood up, stretched their arms and relieved themselves where they stood. Then they covered the fire with earth and lay down for the night. Our team crept up quietly. They did not expect much opposition, as there were two of our men to each opponent, and we also had the advantage of surprise.

Our men crawled right into the hide-out and stood over their sleeping victims. Then they dropped as a leopard would drop from a tree onto a passing buck. But they had underestimated the physical strength of their adversaries. One of our men, Waira, was thrown backwards into the bush. Njeru fell over when his leg was grabbed. Thia, the dwarf, almost lost his revolver. Within seconds knives were flashing, and everyone was wriggling and kicking on the ground in the darkness. A heavy body fell on Njeru's face. He was choking. He gasped, he bit, but all in vain. He was sure he was about to die, so he gave a muffled yell. Waira, bleeding from a knife wound on his arm, broke loose and went to help Njeru. An elbow hit him on the chest and knocked him over. A terrorist dropped on him. Over and over they rolled until the terrorist was under him. This was not a time to worry about bringing them back alive—it was a fight for life. Now Waira's right arm was free. He pulled his knife from its sheath and plunged it deep into his opponent's chest. The man gasped, stretched up a little, then relaxed his grip. Thia was still shouting '*Ninguragwo! Ninguragwo!*' ('I will be killed! I will be killed!'), but Waira could not see him. The dwarf was beneath three or four writhing bodies. Waira pulled the first leg he found, but it did no good.

Then Waira remembered his revolver. He pulled it from its holster inside his skin jacket and fired three shots into the ground. Within seconds the rolling and kicking stopped, and he heard the two remaining terrorists pleading for mercy. It was some time before everyone was able to stand up. Everyone was cut and bleeding.

Unfortunately it was just after these interesting little battles that Tony Lapage was recalled to more routine duties. I doubt whether anyone could have been more sorry to leave us, for his heart and soul were in the job, and he actively enjoyed trailing through those forests day and night with that element of risk always present. Tony was a wonderful companion, who had quite the best sense of humour I have ever known. It was not easy to replace him, and for a long time Gethieya and I carried on alone, but eventually I was joined by Inspector Richard MacLachlan, a slightly built Scotsman from Glasgow, who gloried in a splendid moustache and an extensive knowledge of mechanical and medical matters.

We were closer than we thought, however, to Kahiu
Itina, and after the end of March events occurred in
rapid succession. Our first contact with his gang was on
April Fool's Day, when one of our teams came face to
face with some of his men and merged, unsuspected, with
them. Unfortunately Kahiu Itina was not with them; he
and eleven others were some fifteen miles through the
forest to the east. The group that our men met were setting game snares over a wide area of the northern Aberdares, and the prospects of our team staying with them,
and eventually accompanying them back to Kahiu Itina,
were excellent.

All went extremely well until the night of the 2nd of
April, when the group was fired upon by a pseudo-gang.
In their journey with Kahiu Itina's men, our team had
knowingly, but unavoidably, passed out of the area closed
to operations. When the firing began everyone scattered,
but no casualties were inflicted and the attack was very
half-hearted. By a stroke of good luck one of our men,
named Kibata, tackled and tied up an enormous terrorist from Kahiu Itina's gang called Ruku during the
confusion, and the next morning brought him to a point
in the forest where we were meeting the team. Ruku
knew exactly where the trapping party were to rejoin
Kahiu Itina. He told us that when he last left him, Kahiu
Itina had been in a hide-out on the Ngobit river near
Wuthering Heights and without delay we rushed round
to that side of the mountain.

To everyone's horror, on arrival at Wuthering Heights
after a back-breaking journey up the Elephant Entry
Track—the worst track on the whole Aberdares—Ruku
stubbornly refused to co-operate with us, insisting that he
had not said that Kahiu Itina was on the Ngobit river.
He now claimed no knowledge of his whereabouts and,
though we knew he had been with the gang for over a

year, he swore that he had only met them twenty-four
hours before. Every effort was made to get him to talk
before others from the trapping party could get back to
Kahiu Itina and tell him about the action, but Ruku
remained as stubborn as ever. By the evening of the 3rd
of April he had still not changed his story, so MacLachlan and I took him over while the teams headed for the
Ngobit river to carry out a general search. All Ruku
asked during the next few hours was that we should
shoot him. He wanted to die.

We made ourselves a small shelter on the fringe of the
Moorlands, and while Mac went off to draw water, I
took Ruku with me to gather firewood, which was no
easy task in the darkness. When we had gone a short way
from the camp I told him he could go away if he wished.
I had said this to unco-operative terrorists before, and
found that it had worked wonders. They would, of
course, be very stupid if they did go, as they would certainly be murdered by their confederates, who would suspect them of being won over or bribed by us. Ruku was
astonished. He looked at me menacingly for some moments,
then sat down on the ground and shook his head.

'Where do you want me to go?' he asked.

'Why not go back to Kahiu Itina?' I suggested.

'So you want me to be killed, do you?'

'Haven't you been asking me to kill you for the last
two hours? What does it matter whether I kill you or
Kahiu Itina kills you?'

Ruku realized then that he could not leave us. He
knew that if he were seen again by Kahiu Itina's men
they would kill him. Once he had been missed after the
shooting, the gang would be sure that he was coming
back to betray his leader. That was the Mau Mau way of
thinking. His simple mind suddenly realized that while
his enemy was allowing him his freedom, his friends

would kill him when they saw him again. What an odd world it was! From that moment Ruku's outlook changed. Without a word he rose to his feet and began to look for firewood, and when we had gathered enough and gone back to camp, he lit the fire and fetched stones for us to sit on. As the night passed he became more and more friendly and talkative. By dawn he had volunteered to lead us to the spot where he had last seen Kahiu Itina.

At daybreak, as Mac and I were about to set off with Ruku to hunt Kahiu Itina ourselves, two members of our team arrived unexpectedly at the camp to report. All night they had searched along both banks of the Ngobit river, but had not seen or heard anything, and Gati now wanted to know what to do. As they told their story and described their search, Ruku listened intently. When they had finished he asked:

'Did you reach the place where the muiri tree has fallen?'

'*Aca*, we have seen no muiri tree,' they replied.

'In that case let us go now,' Ruku said. With that he rose to his feet and beckoned the two messengers to follow him. And so they left us. Within an hour they had joined the rest of our force and were approaching a thick patch of forest along the east bank of the Ngobit river, but at least a mile above the point where our team had finally called off their search the previous night. On Ruku's advice the force split up here to surround the patch of forest, and several groups of two men each went round to cover all the buffalo paths coming out of the thicket, for only along these paths could anyone travel at speed. Meanwhile he and Gati pushed their way through the undergrowth towards the middle, hoping to flush Kahiu Itina.

They had only gone about a hundred yards, when one of Kahiu Itina's men walked into our sentry post on a buffalo track and was captured. A second terrorist, however, was lagging some thirty yards behind and had seen his companion pounced upon. He turned round and dashed off through the forest. Backwards and forwards he dodged with one of our men called Gacheru on his heels. Finally he broke out and dashed up a hill past Gati and Ruku. They joined in the chase.

He was a hard man to catch. First Gacheru, tired out, fell back and left Gati and Ruku to continue on their own. The agile terrorist darted from left to right like a hare, and then veered south towards the river, leaping down the slope in great bounds, but he could not shake off his pursuers. He plunged into the river, but the smooth river stones were too slippery. He lost his balance and fell heavily into the water. There, too tired to do anything else, he sat up and raised his hands in surrender.

Unlike Ruku, to whom death had once seemed a pleasant relief, this terrorist was terrified of dying. As he was being dragged out of the water, he pleaded desperately with his captors, telling them that he would show them where Kahiu Itina and many others were hiding if they would only spare his life. He confirmed the information that Ruku had given Gati, that Kahiu Itina had been in the patch of forest where the chase began. Only the day before the gang had moved to another hide-out, but he knew exactly how to find this new rendezvous.

It was important to get to it quickly, because it was likely that some sharp-eyed scout had seen the chase and was already racing to warn Kahiu Itina. There was no time for Gati to gather the rest of his force together. He, Ruku, the prisoner, and Gacheru, who had by now arrived at the river, would have to go on alone and trust in Ngai that they would not be killed.

Fortunately the hide-out was not far off and our party

could soon see it. Near the headwaters of the river an outcrop of massive boulders, each several feet high and weighing several tons, surrounded a single, tall, dry tree. The new hide-out was under this tree, but no one could be seen.

Gati pushed the prisoner in front of him, hoping that the gang would first identify our prisoner and think that he was bringing back some stragglers he had picked up during his brief absence. But our party's approach was not detected, and they reached the boulders without a check.

From there they could hear voices in the hide-out. The terrorists were praying in low voices, and someone, probably a witch-doctor, was mumbling words which were being repeated by the rest of the gang. Gati climbed quietly to the top of the nearest rock, and as he peered over it, his automatic ready in his hand, he saw them praying and heard the familiar words, '*Thaai, Thaaiya, Thaai, Haaaah!*' By this time Ruku had taken the prisoner's simi and was crawling up the same rock to lie beside Gati.

All the men in the hide-out were standing in formation facing Mount Kenya with arms raised shoulder high. Gati pointed his gun at them and ordered them to stand where they were; they turned their heads towards him and gazed into the muzzle of his automatic. But no one moved, no one even dropped his arms.

Then someone in the gang shouted, '*Tigai kuura.*' ('Don't run.') It was the voice of Kingori, the greatest of all Mau Mau witch-doctors on the Aberdares. As the gang stood there with their arms still raised above their shoulders, Kingori and Kahiu Itina came forward and looked up at their captors

'I have had a dream,' said Kingori. 'I dreamt that today Ngai would send someone here who was not an

D*

enemy and he would take us to a place of peace. I have
told all these children of mine about this message from
Ngai, and they are at peace. I know you are the one
Ngai has sent.'

'We too have come for peace,' replied Gati, who was
completely taken aback by the meek and pacific reaction
of the terrorists, and unable to make head or tail of what
Kingori had said about a dream. 'Choose three people
to cut muondwe to tie the hands. Everyone else must sit
down. If the three do not return, that will be a sign of
war, and everyone here will die.'

There was a pause. The gang did not move. They
would not comply with orders from anyone but Kingori.
They would sooner be shot down than sit on the ground
without Kingori's instructions. Then Kingori turned and
faced his followers and passed on the orders and, without murmuring, they complied. Three men climbed over
the rocks to go and cut muondwe. There was an uneasy
silence while they were away. Everyone except Kingori,
whose eyes were closed, stared in bewilderment at Gati
and Ruku. They knew their captors well. They were surprised, but they were not frightened, for Ngai, according to Kingori, had sent them, and because of that there
was something sacred about Gati and Ruku. They did
not hate them; they did not like them; they simply looked
at them. Kingori was praying again to his god on Mount
Kenya. He seemed to be in a trance, unmindful of the
gun pointing at him, not caring what his captors or followers were doing. Only when the three muondwe-
cutters slid down the rocks back into the hide-out did he
shake himself back to full consciousness again. Taking
the strips of muondwe, the forest string, in his own hands,
he began to bind his own men. No one objected. In fact
they held out their hands ready for him. When all but
Kahiu Itina and Kingori himself had been tied, he went

back to stand beneath the rock, looked up at Gati, and asked:

'There are three other children in this forest whom we cannot leave. Spare me to send for them.' But before Gati had time to answer he turned his head to look at the prisoner who had led Gati to the hide-out, and asked him: 'Where is the child you went with to the river?'

Much to Gati's surprise, he then heard his prisoner tell Kingori how his companion had been captured on the buffalo path earlier that morning, a fact of which Gati was completely unaware, although his own men had been responsible. Had he known this before he would never have dashed on to the hide-out with only Ruku and Gacheru. He would have gathered his men together first. He had come on almost single-handed because he thought the second terrorist had got away and was on his way to Kahiu Itina.

As the party set off down the river to rejoin the rest of our team, a small group of Kahiu's men were sent off to find the missing members of the gang who were trapping away to the east. As they left they were told to rendez-vous with Gati and Kingori at an old army fort on Wuthering Heights. Their mission also proved successful, and by late afternoon they had returned with the trap-pers. The total number of terrorists accounted for in this single, uncanny operation was brought to twenty-eight.

Throughout the history of the emergency there had never been an incident quite like this one. Kingori's dream was clearly the only reason for the docile and pas-sive attitude of the gang. In the days which followed we questioned and requestioned the gang as we just could not believe the story. But we found that Kingori had, in fact, done just what he told Gati. The day before the attack on the hide-out he had called them all together and told them how Ngai had spoken to him in a dream. He

had told them how 'Ngai would send messengers of
peace', and that when these messengers came everyone
was to remain quiet 'otherwise Ngai would shake with
anger if anyone fled'. Throughout the night the gang had
sat peacefully in the hide-out 'awaiting Ngai's messengers'. Nobody had slept and nobody had talked.
Every few hours Kingori and Kahiu Itina had made the
others stand and face Mount Kenya and pray so that
'Ngai would see they were prepared'. We listened to
each man's story separately. Kingori may well have invented the tale of his talk with Ngai, but there was no
doubt about what he had told his men. Had it not been
for the dream and Kingori's undisputed power over his
superstitious followers, Gati would certainly have had a
very different reception.

I shall never forget my first sight of this large body of
terrorists. Kahiu Itina was obviously the militant leader.
His eyes were bloodshot from strain, and, unlike all the
others, he was almost bald. He wore an ingeniously made
leopard-skin coat and trousers, a vest tailored from a
piece of old canvas tarpaulin, a decorative colobus monkey-skin hat, a Boy Scout belt and a pair of coarse,
brown gaiters made from the thick hide of a buffalo. He
had the walk of a townsman and spoke with a snarl. He
was clearly one of those who liked everyone running
around him, one whose authority had gone to his head
and, as his record showed, he was a most dangerous
fanatic.

Kingori, on the other hand, was quietly spoken and
outwardly gentle. Never had I seen a man so imbued
with the Mau Mau perversions of the old tribal religion.
He spoke and thought about Ngai all day long. It was
difficult to reconcile this meek-looking, god-fearing individual with the powerful Mau Mau witch-doctor that he
was. Even after his capture he was idolized by his fol-

lowers, who bathed his feet, served his food, deloused his hair, and generally waited upon him as diligently as any Roman slaves ever served their masters. At a glance it was difficult to picture him as a protagonist of extreme violence, as one who had blessed the commission of appalling acts of savagery and inspired those who committed them to repeat them over and over again. He seemed to have neither the physique nor the temperament for that sort of thing. But beneath his clothes of animal skins were several scars gained in bygone battles with the Security Forces. One hand had been permanently deformed by a bullet wound.

The rest of the gang had a mass of bristly, woolly hair, which made them look like walking kitchen mops. They had long, black beards. Their eyes were wide, and they wore an assortment of skin jackets and caps. They carried a variety of weapons. Some were European rifles and revolvers, which they had preserved remarkably well throughout their three and a half years in the forest. Some were home-made guns which had been manufactured with an undisputed ingenuity from lengths of piping, bicycle frames and scraps of wire and metal they had found lying about the countryside, but these were often more dangerous for the man who fired them than the target. Many of the animal skins they wore were also tailored with a degree of ingenuity. None were worn for camouflage or disguise. They were all designed for show or warmth, usually for warmth. The softer skins such as those of the hyrax, otter, tree squirrel or pygmy antelope, were used as inner garments with the hair inside to seal the warmth of the body. The coarser, rougher skins of the eland, the bushbuck and the wild pig were used as outer garments. A large bushbuck skin was enough for one coat or pair of trousers, but thirty to forty hyrax skins would be needed for a single inner jacket. All these skins

had been cut up and sewn together with forest twines or
thin strips of leather, which made the finished article far
more durable and strong than one might imagine. Gang
leaders and witch-doctors were the ones who dressed for
show. All the choicest skins such as leopard, colobus,
cheetah or badger were made into an assortment of show
pieces ranging from peaked caps and arm-bands to belts,
gaiters and shoulder straps. Small portions of these
colourful skins were often sewn onto more ordinary skins
as pockets and insignia of rank. But the beauty of this
clothing was purely visual and none could be kept as
souvenirs. All these clothes stank with a peculiarly penetrating odour. It was not surprising. One terrorist, on
being asked when he had last taken off his skin jacket,
proudly answered, 'Not since the skin dried round my
body.'

Witch-doctor Kingori regarded all Mau Mau in the
forest as 'his children'. Nothing would alter his religious
belief that 'Kinyanjui had been sent by Ngai to collect
the children of the forest together', and he was certain
that the Land Rovers we used to bring the gang out of
the forest were the 'maguru ma Ngai' or 'the Legs of God'.
He had entered the jungle three years before, after ad-
ministering Mau Mau oaths in the reserve, and had predicted that 'rocks of fire would one day fall from the sky
onto the forest'. When the bombing of the jungle began,
the terrorists remembered his prediction and turned to
him for advice. When his subsequent prophecies proved
right his fame was enhanced, but when they proved
wrong they were quickly forgotten and the error was
attributed to the thick forests which had distorted Ngai's
words and prevented him hearing them properly. So his
reputation had grown unimpeded by his mistakes until
all Mau Mau came to regard him, as they did witch-
doctor Muraya, as a 'mutumwo wa Ngai' or Ngai's

disciple. To them his power was complete and decisive and when he dreamed his dreams were infallible, but like most Mau Mau witch-doctors he did not dream often, for 'to converse with Ngai too regularly was likely to annoy him'. He would frequently be pressed by his followers to give them personal news or guidance—about the state of their homes, their chances of recovering from their wounds, whether a raid would be successful or whether a journey would be safe or dangerous, but more often than not he would decline to answer such questions on the ground that he could not contact Ngai, Ngai could only contact him. It was a one-way traffic.

Within a week we realized that neither Kahiu Itina nor witch-doctor Kingori would give us information about Dedan Kimathi. Nothing would make them change their attitude. As soon as his name was mentioned they refused to speak. In fact it turned out that they had no useful information to give. They did not know where Kimathi was nor did they want to know.

Some of our old trusted collaborators then advised us that some of the less important members of Kahiu Itina's gang might come forward with useful information about Kimathi if Kingori and Kahiu Itina were removed. We agreed, and, when these two important terrorists had been handed over to the police for normal action, we turned our attention to the others and heard what they had to say.

The effect of Kingori's and Kahiu Itina's removal was instantaneous. The others became far more co-operative. Several of them had news of Kimathi but, alas, their information was of very little value.

We were told that Kimathi, more than any other terrorist in the forest, had become acutely conscious of the dangers of pseudo-gang operations. Not long before he had sent out messengers to the leaders of all the larger gangs, including Kahiu Itina, to say that from a given date he would kill anyone who came near him 'because he could no longer tell who was a traitor and who was not'. Two of his messengers, who had arrived at Kahiu Itina's camp in early February, knew very well how changeable Kimathi was and how suspicious he had become of everything and everyone. They had seen little point in returning to him and living a life completely cut off from all other terrorists in the forest. As a result they had taken the exceptional course, and it certainly was exceptional for Kimathi's men, who were usually fanatically loyal to their leader, of remaining with Kahiu Itina. Both these messengers, Kinyua and Nderitu, were now in our hands.

From all the information Kahiu Itina's men had been able to gather both from forest letter-boxes and from other terrorists with whom they talked, it was clear that the desertion of these two messengers had infuriated Kimathi. We were told that he had embarked on a ruthless campaign to kill any terrorist who did not belong to his own gang. Now everyone was doubly terrified of him and took every possible precaution to avoid him. For this Kingori and Kahiu Itina hated him, and would never allow his name to be mentioned. They had heard that two small groups of terrorists who had gone to find him had been strangled and hacked to pieces by his henchmen.

A large region of the Aberdare forest had thus become known to everyone in the forest as Kimathi's area, and was not entered under any circumstances. Nobody, we were assured, but his own men knew exactly where he was hiding, but it was virtually certain that he would be somewhere in that forbidden region of the mountain. And we now discovered that the forbidden region had been his favourite haunt since he first entered the forest.

From all this it was quite obvious that neither Kahiu

Itina nor Chege Karobia could possibly get us any closer to our target. We had to be content with a rough description of the Kimathi area, where we would now have to go in search of him. In terms of Kimathi, all we had been able to gain from the capture of Kahiu Itina and his gang was information which narrowed down our field of search. From his two deserter messengers, however, we were able to find out a great deal more about his forest life. They told us that he never stayed more than a few hours in one place. Often he would tell his men that he was going north when, in fact, he went south. He was reputed to know more about bushcraft and the forest than any other terrorist, and to be able to travel at considerable speed for seven days without food. It was said that he had such a keen instinct that were he to sit up suddenly during the night and say, 'We go,' as sure as dawn the Security Forces would arrive at the spot within a matter of hours. This mysterious sense which forewarned him of danger was his principal hold on his followers. Despite his vile temper, despite his lust for killing, despite his treacherous, unpredictable temperament, they believed there was more room for survival with him than away from him.

The area in which he had isolated himself had been soundly chosen. It was the part of the Aberdares known as the Tree Tops Salient or Ruthaithi, and the vast forest area to the north-west known as the Mwathe. This part of the mountain, over two hundred square miles in size, was the most difficult and dangerous of all areas on the Aberdares in which to operate. The ridges were steep and the bushes particularly thick, while it contained nearly seven times as many wild animals to the square mile as did any other part of the Aberdare or Mount Kenya forests. After many months of bombing by the R.A.F. the animals were extremely aggressive.

This news depressed us and made us realize that the hunt would be far longer and more difficult than we had originally thought, but we derived some satisfaction from knowing that all three of our initial letter points had either been in or on the edge of this particular area. This showed that our original estimate of Kimathi's whereabouts had not been very wide of the mark. Now we were certain that he had heard the sky-shouts, but it was equally certain that he would never have acted upon them. Nevertheless what we had lost on the swings we had gained on the roundabouts, for as a result of the sky-shout, Gati had come into our hands; through him we had raised a valuable force of terrorists who alone had the knowledge and ability to hunt Kimathi; through them we had accounted for Kahiu Itina and his gang, and lastly we had been able to narrow down our field of search to an area covering less than one-tenth of the Aberdare mountain.

Now that we knew why Kingori and Kahiu Itina hated Kimathi, Gethieya, Gati and I decided to visit them in the prison to see whether their new surroundings had loosened their tongues. First we went to see Kahiu Itina. We were there but a few minutes. Imprisonment, to put it mildly, had not improved his temper or his temperament. Next we went to see Kingori. As we entered his cell we found him facing Mount Kenya, praying to his god, Ngai. He stopped abruptly when the door was unlocked.

'This is better than the forest, is it not, Kingori?' I asked him.

'*Muno, muno*,' ('Much, much better,') he answered. 'Ngai has already spoken to me here and I am happy.'

'What did he say, Kingori?' I inquired.

He shook his head, then closed his eyes for a few seconds before looking at me again. 'He told me all the

children in the forest will leave soon, all but Kimathi.
He will be finished. He will be arrested in the tenth
month before the rains for the millet planting begin.'

The tenth month, I thought—that is October. It was
still April. Another six months! 'There is nothing which
will keep Kimathi in that forest for another six months,
Kingori,' I assured him. We talked for some minutes
more, then I left.

We now trained our sights onto the Tree Tops Salient
and the Mwathe. For the first time we experienced in full
measure the ordeal of operating in this particular region
during the seasonal long rains, which broke in full fury
at exactly this moment.

Chapter Nine

THE LONG RAINS BREAK

Oi, oi, egunaga ki?

What is the use of crying 'Oi, oi'?

or

What cannot be cured must be endured.

THE long rains, which begin with tremendous force at the end of March or beginning of April, usually go on without any real pause for the first week, then taper off into spasmodic afternoon thunderstorms.

Within minutes of the first deafening clap of thunder, the rough forest tracks become quagmires and everything, everywhere, is drenched. Frightened by the lightning and thunder, the larger animals come out onto the tracks and wallow in the mud, tearing deep craters with their feet and making travel yet more difficult.

These heavy rains are often preceded by hailstorms of great violence which tear leaves and even branches from trees, destroy the beautiful wild flowers, drive the animals frantic and cover the ground with a white, pebbled crust.

Most of the vehicle tracks in the Aberdares—and there are few paths that qualify for this modest title—are built on the side of ridges. The ridge tops are too narrow for tracks and the bottoms are usually filled by streams. When the earth is heavy with hail or rainwater, landslides are a constant danger. When the rains are over we always had to send large working gangs up into the forest to grub away the piles of broken earth or rebuild those bits of track which had been swept away altogether. Throughout the rainy season, in fact, a vehicle is of little use, and if you want to travel you have to walk. Even walking is a tricky business. Within hours of the rain starting all the little streams swell and become formidable barriers. In their swirling waters there are bits of dry wood, broken logs and even tree stumps. These are difficult to see in the brown, muddy water and they sometimes cause severe injury to man and beast alike. Detours of fifteen or twenty miles are sometimes necessary in a journey that would normally cover less than three miles.

Then there are the animals. Terrified by the thunder, they charge to and fro in a constant and hostile challenge to any intruder in their kingdom. The Mau Mau used to say that the animals associated thunder with bombing, and that during thunderstorms they became crazed with fear. Certainly I had never before seen game react during thunderstorms as they did on the Aberdares after the bombing. Elephant, rhino and buffalo would crash wildly through the bush as if trying to escape from their shadows; warthog and bushbuck would race aimlessly backwards and forwards; and even the monkeys would leap down from their branches and huddle together in frightened little groups at the foot of the trees. The terrorists reported that monkeys sometimes used to come down from the treetops and lie beside them at the bottom of the large, heavy trees as soon as the drone of an aeroplane was heard. Like the Mau Mau they had learnt by costly experience that the sound of an aircraft or the explosion of a bomb was a signal to seek cover, and that there was no better cover than the trunks of the larger trees. As long as the drone of the aircraft's engines continued, these little creatures would lie side by side with the Mau Mau oblivious of their presence. After the bombing I often saw the monkeys take shelter beneath trees at the first sound of thunder.

The rains had a most depressing effect on those of us who were not really used to living in the jungle. There can be few experiences in this world more demoralizing than sitting out in the pouring rain hour after hour unable to find dry shelter, surrounded by thick, cold forest, and knowing that the discomfort has to be endured for a long while to come. Then your morale receives its ultimate test, for there is nothing to distract your mind from the present misery, no imminent danger, no chance of action, no one to talk to, for even if you have a companion the noise of the rain is too loud. There is nothing to do but sit or lie and feel the rain trickling through your clothes. Despondently, you look first at the dark sky above, then at the drooping leaves, each one of which is making its contribution to the flooding river thundering down the valley below. This is the time when small things are your only consolation. Your eye rests on an ant dashing up and down a twig floating in a pool. The plight of the little insect stimulates a morbid curiosity and you watch it for minutes, wondering when it will be swept away to its doom. Then you suddenly feel sorry for it and fish the twig gently out of the puddle so that the ant can crawl away to safety. Or your eye is attracted to a particular leaf from which water is dropping with monotonous regularity. You count the drops until this seems futile, and then your thoughts return again to the cold and misery of everything.

The rain continues into the night. Then the thunder rumbles and, as it fades away, you hear the trumpeting of frightened elephants. Sometimes they are so near that their trumpeting is almost as loud as the thunder. You wonder which way they are moving and whether it will be possible to hear them above the noise of the rain if they get really close. Then the thunder stops and the elephants are silent. Only the patter of the raindrops and the roar of the torrent in the valley below break the hush of the forest, from which all the familiar noises have vanished.

I usually found that the best distraction came from a group of friendly terrorists. Hardened to all discomforts they showed no reaction to rain, heat or cold. They never worried about being hungry or cold or wet through to the skin. I watched them sleep soundly on a saturated layer of leaves and twigs with rain pouring straight down on them. They would wake up fresh and cheerful ready for another day of dampness. With the terrorists pride became your strongest ally.

Yet when the rain stops your spirits soon rise and life in the forest seems better than ever. The sun brings warmth, and the birds come out, the trees begin to stir in the breeze, shaking off the rainwater trapped in their leaves, and the little buck come out into the glades to frisk and get warm. The musty gases rise from the compost and mulch to mingle with the odour of sweet-smelling cape chestnut trees, giving the forest an aroma of its own. Everywhere there is beauty in abundance and a freshness of life. Everything is great and majestic and remote from the rush and noise of civilization. Here there is nothing to see or hear, but nature in its naked form, unspoilt by man. This, one realizes, is paradise. It is the land of mountains and rivers and trees and all things wild, but it is a wonderful land, and God is good.

Before the rains come the terrorists prepare themselves. They know that it is difficult to conceal your tracks when the ground is wet; so they gather as much food as they can and store it away in caves and hollowed-out trees; they lift their game traps and rig them up nearer to their hide-outs; they hunt for honey and, after collecting enough to see them over the wet season, roll it in thick animal skins to prevent badgers getting at it.

Before the rain pelts down and the rivers run high, they also move their hide-outs away from the bigger streams and set them up again beside little springs, for they know that the noise made by rivers in flood will drown the sound of an approaching enemy. They put their hide-outs in parts of the forest where rain or hail will not flatten the undergrowth, and where the ground is covered with a thick bed of leaves and bark which will mask their footprints when they go out to visit their game traps, their letter boxes, or their food stores. They know that elephant and rhino will now come down the mountain towards the low farming country in their seasonal migration to feed on the young, green crops. During this migration the animals will churn up all the places where there are natural salt-licks, pools of water or patches of muondwe. All these places have to be avoided therefore when new hide-outs are being chosen.

They know, too, that even if they have plenty of honey, it will still be necessary to trap buck for meat. All places in the jungle where a shrub called magomboki is growing will be bad for trapping, for, soon after the beginning of the rains, this will become so thick and matted that buck will not pass through it. New trapping areas where there is no magomboki have to be found.

They also have to think about firewood. Wood dampened by rain will give out too much smoke, and they know that smoke is dangerous, for it helps their enemies to find them. They must, therefore, have their hide-outs in or near the bamboo belt, as bamboo is their ideal firewood, whether wet or dry.

While the rains do not bring about any change in terrorist morale, they do cause a marked change in their mode of living. Like a snake, they recoil and are harder to see. Like a mushroom, they shrivel up, change colour and become invisible in the seedbed. Yet for those who have lived through these seasonal changes and who know the factors which govern the Mau Mau moods and moves, rain simplifies the hunt. It did for our collaborators. They were able to write off all parts of the forest where magomboki grew in quantity, where there were pools and salt-licks and fast-running rivers, where the vegetation was flimsy and where there were elephant walks and where muondwe thrived. They knew the Mau Mau would be near springs where the water was silent and clean, where bushbuck and duiker could be trapped, where bamboo firewood could be found, and where there were trees which shed their leaves.

With all this and more knowledge in their heads, our collaborators were able to narrow down the Kimathi area very considerably until we had a target area of about fifty square miles to concentrate in. Unfortunately this new smaller target area consisted of no less than eight small portions of forest. Kimathi could be in any one of them.

Three of these were in the western sector, the Mwathe. The remaining five were in the eastern, the Tree Tops Salient. The more we studied the matter, the more we realized that it was impossible to search for him in them all simultaneously. We only had enough men to operate in five areas at once, and even five was stretching us to the limit. We therefore planned a deception operation, to chase him out of any of the three areas in the Mwathe into any of the five areas in the Tree Tops where hunting conditions were slightly better. We would try and frighten him by firing machine-guns in the western region. The shots would be heard by Kimathi, if he were there, and he would imagine that a major operation had been mounted. This would send him scurrying down to the Tree Tops Salient.

There was no question of installing ourselves in the five Tree Tops areas before all the noise was made in the west. We knew that if we were to move in before he came down, he would not come down at all. This may seem extraordinary, but there was good reason for it. We knew how difficult it was to conceal our own tracks in the jungle, how much more difficult it would be to conceal them from that expert Kimathi, and how the whole idea would be wrecked if he happened to see the tracks we had left while moving in. He would double back, and wherever he went he would remain on the alert. Moreover, it was a foregone conclusion that if our deception plan did succeed in chasing him down into the Tree Tops, he would spend the first two days searching through the forest to see if the area was clear and safe. During that time he or his men would be certain to find evidence of our presence. But if we stayed out until he had completed his check and settled down, our chances of making contact with him would be much greater. His sentry lines would be shorter, he would cook and he would put out his game traps. This would help us to find him.

It was pelting with rain when we mounted the first phase of our operation. Slipping and sliding along in the mud we had to use both our hands to cling onto the bamboo poles. This was my first experience of operating in those particular parts of the Mwathe forest during the rains and I shall never forget it. The place was teeming with rhino. Forest rhino are seldom seen in more than twos, but on that day we found them in groups of up to eight. Every few hundred yards there would be a snort, followed by another snort as the massive beasts came hurtling down on us with their ears flattened against their heads and their horns ripping out the vegetation in front of them. It was a nightmare! After the first two or

three narrow escapes, we found it far safer to drop everything and take to the trees as soon as the first snort was
heard. As we moved along our eyes darted from one tree
to another in an anxious search for those we could climb
without too much difficulty. We had our guns in our
hands, and this meant that we could not grab the
bamboo with both hands. Every few yards someone was
falling down, and the noise of our stumbling and falling
made it very difficult to hear the snorts of the rhino. As
the timing of the firing was carefully synchronized, I
had made a point of stressing to our men that there was
to be no shooting under any circumstances until zero
hour. After being put to flight several times in the
first mile by charging rhino, I deeply regretted having
said this. Our 9 mm. Patchett automatics would have
been little better than pea-shooters against rhino, but
their loud clatter might have frightened the beasts
away.

Our agile terrorists were natural experts at dodging
and tree climbing, which usually meant that Mac and I
reached the trees well behind them, and could only hoist
ourselves off the ground by clutching at their wet skin
clothes and pulling ourselves up or pulling them down.
They said it was only because 'we did not smell of the
forest', as they did, that the rhino charged us so frequently, and although I never knew how much truth
there was in this, I suspected that they might be right.
When they operated alone they seldom had trouble with
game. On the other hand, it was likely that the rain was
the cause of the rhinos' ferocity. How, I wondered, could
any terrorist survive for long in this murderous region.
After all the bombing and strafing of the forests there were
a great many wounded animals about. Now their injuries
had healed, but the pain they had gone through had
turned them into ill-tempered rogues.

This was certainly one of those rare days when everything was against us. The rain was unusually heavy, so heavy in fact that each drop stung slightly as it landed on our arms and faces; the going was painfully hard, and our various guides seemed quite incapable of avoiding the many patches of wild nettle, which covered our arms, faces and legs with ugly, inflamed rashes. The design of our Patchetts did not improve our tempers. With 'arms' and 'legs' jutting out from all sides, this gun either catches on branches and delays your retreat, or jabs you severely in the ribs or stomach as you run away.

Despite the trials, however, the operation went off according to plan, and at exactly mid-day the first loud burst of firing rang through the forest. Then at five-minute intervals for the next half-hour firing continued at different points throughout the area. The noise echoed and thundered down the deep gorges. If any Mau Mau were in the region, they would not be there long.

After each volley the elephant could be heard trumpeting and schools of monkeys leapt frantically from the trees into the bamboo undergrowth beneath. There is something mysterious about the sound of gunfire in the jungle. Not only do the reports seem much louder, but they awaken within you the thought that every living creature for miles and miles is on the alert and terrified, and this makes you feel unnerved and faintly guilty.

With this operation completed, the stage was now set for our first offensive against Dedan Kimathi and his fifty dangerous adherents. We were ready—and anxious.

Chapter Ten

A SHARP REBUFF

Riu ni thatu, no riu ringi
ni mbura ya mahiga

Today it is misty, but afterwards
it will rain hailstones

or

Stormy days lie ahead.

ON the 18th of April 1956 the finishing touches were put
to the planning and preparations of our first direct operation against Dedan Kimathi and his gang. Twenty-two
of our terrorists had been specially selected for the operation. They were those who knew every member of
Kimathi's gang, those who knew the ground in the Tree
Tops Salient best, those who were the best trackers and
those who were completely trustworthy, battle-hardened
and brave.

These men were to operate in two teams, each eleven
strong. Four men in each were to be armed with automatic weapons, while the balance were to carry pistols
and simis and one or two home-made guns, for effect.
Their rations had been securely packed away in their
animal-skin bags, and their leaders had carefully checked
their clothing for anything which might give them away
—a match, pieces of paper and the many other things
which they could easily pick up when outside the forest.
A strong-smelling native tobacco called kiraiku, used by
Mau Mau in the forest, was rubbed over their bodies to

drown any non-forest smells, and all traces of dust were brushed away, as there is no dust in the Aberdares. Their simis and knives were splattered with goat's blood, because no knife in the forest is clean.

This odd and somewhat frightening array of Mau Mau was assembled in a tent at our Mayfield base, where I explained to them which areas we had sealed off for our operations, and which were still open to normal Security Force operations and therefore dangerous for them to enter. I explained where Mac, Gethieya and I would go each day to rendezvous with them, where in the forest we would base ourselves, and how they were to identify themselves to us, and we to them, in the event of our running into one another unexpectedly. I emphasized that their task was not to get Kimathi this time, for we realized this was impossible while so many terrorists were guarding him. Our aim was to snatch one or more of his henchmen without the rest of the gang knowing of our snatch. We would then withdraw quickly to one of the pre-arranged rendezvous and try to win over whoever had fallen into our hands. It was unnecessary for me to say any more to our men. All specific points such as how the two teams would work and liaise with one another, what they would do in the event of a battle or a chase, how they would approach their target areas and what they would do if they came upon any game trap, letter boxes or food stores, were left to them to sort out among themselves. In my experience it merely confused these unusual people if a European interfered in such matters. Their ideas about tactics were poles apart from ours, and their methods were strange. The issue boiled down to this—the Mau Mau knew their own kind, and the jungle in which they lived.

After I had said my few words, one of the team leaders moved into the middle of the tent and gathered all those

taking part in the operation round him in a circle. With
legs crossed and weapons on their laps, they sat down for
the conference as they had done a hundred times
before in the forest. When a team leader or an ordinary
team member spoke, he would hold in his left hand a
number of thin sticks about a foot long, and as he made
a point or said something important, he would take
one of the sticks in his right hand and flick it onto the
ground.

Gati was the first to speak. 'You, Njeru,' he said, 'you
cross the ford with Hungu's mbutu [gang or team] and
go through the Mathakwa-ini area.' This was his first
point, so he flicked a stick onto the ground. 'But where
the black forest and bamboo meet, watch the ridge which
goes down towards the place where the grass was burnt.'
Down went another stick.

'*Noguo*,' answered Njeru, picking up the two sticks to
signify that both points were understood. Now Njeru
came into the centre, and as he flicked a stick onto the
ground he said to another, Wanjau, 'You know the
place where we turn before the river, where there is a
tree which has had all its bark scraped off by an elephant, nobody should pass there.'

'There is nobody here who doesn't know it,' interrupted one of the listeners, picking up Njeru's stick.

Then Ruku took over a bundle of the sticks and went
into the middle. 'There is a place where they used to trap
hyrax among some munderendu trees—you can see
Chania hill from there and the waterfall on the Gura can
be heard.'

'By the little bluff?' inquired Kibata.

'*Aca*, further on a little where the muondwe reaches
here,' replied Ruku, holding his throat.

'Yes, we know it,' chimed several voices.

'Well,' said Ruku, casting down a stick, 'behind there

we should be very careful, because they might be there
and it is impossible to cover up tracks.'

'*Noguo, noguo,*' everyone agreed.

For nearly two hours this mysterious discussion continued, with sticks being thrown down and picked up in
strict, ceremonial order. They talked about places where
a certain type of tree had fallen, where such and such a
terrorist's trap had broken, where ammunition used to be
hidden in an elephant's skull, where two waterfalls could
be heard at the same time; they talked about a well-
known place for finding kirangi, a type of fungus which
grows around bamboo poles and is used for medicinal
purposes, where a certain very important spring was
situated, and where there were poisonous plants; they
even talked about 'a valley of echoes' and the whistling
calls of the night birds. To us it was incomprehensible,
but their system worked. With no set order of speaking,
for the procedure allowed anyone to speak whenever he
wanted, they were able to have a full exchange of views
and ideas. This meant that every detail was thoroughly
understood and examined before it was passed. But the
rules were strict. No one uttered a word before the
speaker had finished his point, unless he was not clear
about something. Only when a stick had been thrown to
the ground could another man rise to say his bit. If three
men wanted to speak simultaneously, there would be no
scramble for a stick; the terrorist nearest to the stick
would have priority, and the others would not argue
about it. They knew their turn would come in good
time. In any case their system was such that there was
every chance of someone else making their points for
them, because from the beginning to the end the emphasis was on thoroughness. But there was another reason
for the customary restraint shown in the picking-up of
sticks—a stick was only cast down to mark essential and

PSEUDO-TERRORISTS PLAITING ONE ANOTHER'S HAIR TO
FACILITATE THE REMOVAL OF LICE

TEAM LISTENING TO THE ALARM CALLS OF THE NDETE
BIRD DURING OPERATIONS

INSIDE THE BAMBOO
IN THE ZAINA VALLEY

KIMATHI'S FAVOURITE
'PRAYER TREE' IN
THE MWATHE VALLEY,
WHICH FELL WITHIN
A MATTER OF HOURS
OF HIS CAPTURE

important points in a speech. Unless a point was important enough to warrant a stick, it was not important
enough to be mentioned at all. If a terrorist tried to talk
too long, and if the points he was making did not warrant
the sticks he was throwing down, he would have his
sticks taken away from him. This was a severe humilia-
tion, and one which marked the offender as a person
unsuited 'to be among men'. If this happened in the
forest, he might be thrown out of the gang. This rule had
the effect, therefore, of restricting debate to only the main
and essential issues. It also dissuaded all but the most
foolhardy from standing up and talking a lot of nonsense.

When the time eventually came to rise, when everything that was to be said had been said, and when all the
sticks lay on the ground and nobody wanted to pick one
up, Gati moved into the centre of the circle again.
Moving his finger slowly round the gathering like the
hand of a clock, he asked all present, 'Have we arrived
at the roots?'

'Yes,' chanted the audience. 'At the ones which reach
down to the rocks.'

That was the end of the affair. They had dealt with it
from its highest branches all the way down to its lowest
roots, the roots which reach to the rocks.

Long after dark that night the teams made their way
silently into the forest. They set off from our transport
in one long line. Each one of them shook hands with us
as they left, but only Gati and Hungu spoke. These two
team leaders had quite a lot to say at that final moment,
and as they talked on and on, I wondered how they
could ever hope to catch up with their teams again. This
did not worry them, however. They knew the answers.
When they too had gone, Mac, Gethieya and I drove on
in the darkness without using our lights until we reached
the point where the track entered the forest, and there

E

we left our vehicles. That same night the three of us tramped many miles through the forest until we reached the place where we were to rendezvous later with our teams.

For the first thirty-six hours the hunt was uneventful. Four of the likely areas in the salient were searched, but without result. The fifth we avoided because there were too many noisy Sykes monkeys about, and we feared that they would betray the hunters by their calls. We visited every spot where Kimathi had camped in the days when Kinyua (one of the two messengers who had deserted and joined Kahiu Itina) had been in the gang, but no trace of Kimathi was found anywhere.

On the afternoon of the second day the teams met at a pre-arranged point in the forest, and a council of war was held. Here it was decided that Hungu's team would cut across the salient to the Ruhotie valley in the north, while Gati would go back with his men to the area they had previously avoided because of the Sykes monkeys. Gati had a strong urge to go there, as not only was it the only one of the five target areas they had not been to, but he suspected that the cunning Kimathi might lie up close to the trees full of Sykes monkeys, so that they could warn him if anyone entered the region. He had been known to shadow game before in order to protect himself. During operation 'Sledgehammer', when large numbers of troops and police assisted by tribal police and Kikuyu loyalists had swept through the forests, he had tailed a small herd of elephants, knowing that the animals would not wander through parts of the jungle where the Security Forces were operating, and that even if they did encounter a patrol, the elephants would raise the alarm. And so the two teams parted. Throughout the operation they did not come into contact with one another again.

The area for which Gati now set course was known to the Mau Mau as Kahare-ini because of the unusually large number of tree squirrels which live there. To reach it he had to cross three rivers, and after the rains there were only two or three fords on each which were still passable. While the team was crossing the third of these rivers, the Itha, round about mid-day on the 21st of April, the first evidence of Kimathi's presence was found. On the southern bank, where buffalo had watered and churned up the muddy ground, they saw the tracks of a sizeable gang. The tracks were very fresh, certainly not more than three hours old, and in the tracks were several distinct impressions made by a pair of sandals cut out of an old motor-car tyre. One of the very few terrorists who owned such sandals was Wambararia, Kimathi's brother.

For some distance from the river the tracks were easy to follow. The gang knew that when it was dark, herds of buffalo would come down to the water and churn up the ground once again with their hooves. But after about a mile they branched off the buffalo path which they were following. Now the trail was well hidden, and it was only after Gati and his men had studied the tracks for many minutes that they discovered the gang had split into two groups. Gati decided to divide up his team and follow both.

This proved to be unwise, for after following one set of the tracks some short distance, the smaller of our two units, the one that Gati was not with, suddenly found they had stumbled onto a hide-out, and were being watched by some of Kimathi's well-armed gangsters. As our men walked on, blissfully unaware of their danger, Kimathi's men aimed their guns.

Finally one of the gangsters shouted: 'Stand where you are, and send one man up.'

It was Jeriko, one of Kimathi's lieutenants. Everyone in our little team froze with fright. They saw they were covered by the rifles of the gang; they knew they were far outnumbered, and they knew that it would be suicide for them to run.

After some prompting and nudging the leading collaborator, whose name was Kingarua, went forward unwillingly. He was shivering with fright. He walked forward slowly and stopped beside a smouldering fire in the centre of the hide-out. '*Tutiri na uuru!*' ('We have nothing bad!') he said repeatedly as he stood there, but there was no response.

Then after a few minutes, Jeriko's voice suddenly blurted out again. 'What are you looking for, you ticks?'

'*Aca*,' replied Kingarua. 'We are only looking for others.'

'Which others?'

'*Aca*,' answered Kingarua. 'Only others who were with us when we went to find food in the reserve.'

Again there was a long silence. Kingarua felt like running, but he knew he would be the first to be killed if he did so. He wanted to look back to make sure that his companions were still there, but he felt this might make the gangsters think that he was planning to make a break and that would also mean his death. Behind him our men were breathing easier, for they reckoned that if Jeriko had not believed Kingarua he would have opened fire long ago.

For five minutes nothing happened. There was not a sound from the forest. Kingarua once thought he heard someone whispering, but he was not sure. Then there was a loud rustling in the bushes about twenty yards ahead of Kingarua and Jeriko stepped out carrying a .303 rifle. Three other terrorists, all armed, were close behind him. They bore down on poor Kingarua, who was sure that his last day had come.

'What I have told you is true, Jeriko, because if I was lying we would have run away,' pleaded Kingarua.

'I am not arguing,' replied Jeriko, who came right up to Kingarua before stopping within a yard of him and dropping the butt of his rifle on the ground. 'Who are the ones you are looking for?' he asked.

Kingarua thought fast. He had to invent a story. He began telling Jeriko how he had left the Moorlands four days before and gone down to the Kikuyu reserve to find food; how they had asked some old women working on their plots along the forest edge to fetch them some potatoes; how these women had run away screaming, and how, after this, he and his companions had moved further down the forest edge until they were opposite a large banana plantation. On and on Kingarua talked. Like all Mau Mau, he knew how to spin out a yarn, and would come to the point only if he was pressed to do so. He knew that if he talked for long enough in a convincing way, the question he had been asked would probably be forgotten altogether. He was still talking when Jeriko interrupted.

'Ssst!' he silenced Kingarua. He had heard the drone of a Piper Pacer aircraft. The noise grew louder and louder. It seemed to be coming overhead.

The aircraft was not connected with our operation, but Kimathi's suspicious men instantly thought in terms of air support for ground forces, probably a supply drop for a pseudo-gang. Something, they thought, was up. Their reaction was swift. Kingarua was grabbed, hit on the head, and thrown to the ground. Some of Jeriko's men jumped from their hiding-places and charged up the hill towards the rest of our men. One of them fired at Kin-

garua lying on the ground. Others fired at the group.
Our men threw themselves down in the grass, pulled out
their Patchett guns, which had been hidden under their
skin garments, and fired burst after burst in rapid succession at the men around Kingarua.

The weight of the fire must have come as a great shock
to the gangsters, who had not even seen any of the weapons carried by our men. Like leaves in a wind eddy they
scattered into the forest. Everything was over in those
few seconds. The gang had vanished into the jungle, but
behind them they had left one of Kimathi's so-called
brigadiers named Thurura, who was lying groaning
beside the fire with a bullet wound in his back. Our men
could see that Thurura was too badly injured to move.
They were sure that they must have hit some others and
rushed forward into the forest after the gang. There was
a running fight. Now and then they caught fleeting
glimpses of Kimathi's men and fired at them. Every few
hundred yards Kimathi's men paused to shoot back. For
nearly three-quarters of an hour—and over four miles—
the plucky little group were on the heels of their enemy.
Several hundred rounds were fired and the noise was tremendous. Eventually, fearing they would run out of ammunition, our men broke off and ran back to the hide-out
to collect Thurura.

Gati was waiting for them when they got back. He and
his section had arrived a few minutes before. The set of
tracks he had followed took him to the same hide-out, but
they had been too late for the battle. All they had seen
were the empty cartridge cases lying about and a trail of
blood leading from the fire to a thick patch of thornbush.
Gati had followed the trail and as he parted the thorny
branches with the muzzle of his gun, he had seen
Thurura, the wounded brigadier, stuffing a wad of documents into his mouth. Gati had jumped in, prised

Thurura's mouth open with a sheath knife, and pulled out the half-chewed documents before Thurura could swallow them.

Supported by a man on either side, Thurura was carried away that afternoon, and by dusk the team had gone a long way towards the rendezvous where we were to meet them. At their resting-place in the forest that night, the wretched Kingarua, who had so narrowly escaped death at the hands of Kimathi's gang during the day, stubbornly insisted that it was his personal right to strangle Thurura without delay. He kept on trying to carry out his threat until he was warned that he would be shot unless he kept silent. When he heard this he spat several times on the ground in utter disgust, and then walked away from our team. He spent the night sitting alone under a tree, muttering periodical threats that he would definitely strangle Thurura one day.

Round the fire that night Thurura was questioned thoroughly. Every time he spoke a word the ill-tempered Kingarua would shout out, 'All that is lies. He should be buried!' But Thurura paid no attention to him. Quietly he told his story. The group he had been with was seventeen strong, and had not included Kimathi, who was about five miles further east with the rest of his gang when the firing broke out. He would certainly have received news of the action by now, even had he not heard the shooting, so there was no point in following him. Thurura spent the night handcuffed to a tree, while the team dozed in a circle round him. At first light they set off to meet us at the rendezvous, carrying him on a bamboo stretcher.

By the time Thurura reached us he was in very poor shape and Kingarua, needless to say, was delighted. The wound in Thurura's back had bled profusely all night.

He was semi-delirious. From the colour of the blood he was coughing up, it was clear that the bullet had passed through his lungs. He was so far gone that he was quite unable to show any concern when the malevolent Kingarua returned to the attack and asked me, in Thurura's hearing, whether he could now strangle him. Mac immediately got down to first aid and dressed the wound most expertly. I had often meant to ask him, because his knowledge of medicine always astounded me, why he had chosen the police as a career when he could have found a more lucrative, and certainly more comfortable, occupation as a doctor.

Thurura was tough. With some brandy down his throat, some food in his stomach, and his wound cleaned and dressed, he revived amazingly quickly. After two or three hours he insisted on sitting up and talking. He told us that we should swing our operations into the Mwathe region where we had previously staged the deception operation, which, incidentally, he said had worked like a magic wand. That was where Kimathi would now return. On the strength of this, we withdrew both teams from the Tree Tops Salient, and spent the next three days unsuccessfully searching through the Mwathe forest. We were pestered by rhino and found in the end that we had been led onto a false trail. Thurura knew Kimathi would not go back up there so quickly, and had misled us deliberately to give his leader more time to get away. This amused me more than it did Kingarua, who once again talked of strangling Thurura. To him this was the last straw. He became so preoccupied with the thought of murder that we had to segregate him and keep him under watch for some time to come.

Although half Gati's team had been compromised in the eyes of Kimathi's gang by this engagement, and could not be used against the gang again, we were not too disappointed with the result of this first operation. The documents pulled out of Thurura's mouth showed that Kimathi was loath to leave the Tree Tops Salient and the Mwathe as Kahiu Itina's men had told us. In fact, one particular document—a letter he had scribbled to Jeriko a few days before—ordered Jeriko not to leave these two areas 'even if the enemy came like a swarm of locusts'. Another note told Jeriko to be at a point on the Kinaini river on a certain date 'because the District Commissioner would be coming to tea!!'

Thurura, however, gave us a depressing account of Kimathi's tactics and precautions, which he genuinely believed were fool-proof. He politely refused to concede that secretly capturing any of his men was a practicable proposition. 'Even if Kimathi is eventually killed or captured,' Thurura insisted, 'he will be the last terrorist in the Aberdares.'

This was our first engagement with the gang, or more accurately with part of it, and discussion on the topic ran high for several days. Many of our men who came from Nyeri district, to which Kimathi himself belonged, seemed less enthusiastic about the idea of hunting him now that it was clear that he had so much ammunition. They believed that if Kimathi had been with Jeriko during the fight, his men would have fought even more ferociously, and our small team would have been shot to pieces. The attitude of our men from the Fort Hall district, on the other hand, was quite different. They thought Jeriko's flight was a sign that the gangsters were not as resolute as they had thought, and this led our Fort Hall men to think that if they were very well armed themselves, they could deal with the gang. Because of this split in our ranks, we decided we would try to use as many Fort Hall terrorists as possible against Kimathi in subsequent operations. It was, after all, the Fort Hall

E*

people who had borne the brunt of Kimathi's savagery in the forest.

The question of whether or not Gati had been right to split up his team was debated at great length by our terrorists. The majority held the view that in future it would be preferable to risk losing contact and keep our teams intact, rather than divide up into small, vulnerable groups. I was fully in agreement with this. I didn't want to lose any of our own Mau Mau or the firearms we had issued to them. We could not afford to add to our risks by committing small units against Kimathi's powerful gang.

It was also agreed that on all future occasions one member of our teams would travel several yards in front to reduce the risk of the whole team being pinned down and compromised as was the case in the action with Jeriko. There were the usual jokes when some far-thinking individual asked whether he could bring up the rear in future.

Naturally the Piper Pacer came in for severe criticism. 'It is very bad,' said Waira, 'for anyone to come and flap his wings and dangle his legs near Kimathi, because he might become so annoyed he will finish us all.' I arranged with the appropriate authorities that 'nobody would flap his wings and dangle his legs' over any area in which we were operating from then onwards.

Chapter Eleven

KIMATHI REACTS

Karakunywo niko koi kwigita

He who is pinched knows how
to defend himself

or

Scalded cats fear even cold water.

THE news of the battle with Jeriko came as a great shock
to Kimathi. He was sitting alone reading his Kikuyu ver-
sion of the Old Testament when the first man to get back
from the fight came running up to his sentries and gave
the alarm. Kimathi jumped up, and without waiting to
hear more of the details, disappeared into the forest as
fast as his legs could carry him, leaving his Bible on the
ground. By the time Jeriko and the rest of his followers
arrived Kimathi was a long way away, threading a
course through the forest which kept him mostly on his
hands and knees.

For two whole days his men looked for him, visiting
the letter boxes they thought he might use, the places
he had said he liked, the game-traps from which he
might have taken a dead buck to eat, but there was no
sign of him anywhere. On the night of the second day, as
some of his searchers were quietly warming themselves
round a fire in a particularly thick patch of forest near
the Muringato river, his high-pitched, almost feminine,
voice cut through the darkness, 'Name all those with
you!'

His brother, Wambararia, stood up and gave his own name, then the names of the five others who were with him.

'There is Abdalla, whom you know because of his thin legs; Ngunyi, the one with a broken sheath for his knife; Gitahi, the child who is fierce; Mbaka, who was sick when you left. Only Karau remains. He brought the honey from the Zaina. There are no others. We have been looking for you.'

When Kimathi heard this he was satisfied, for he knew the details were correct and he recognized the voice of his brother. Coming straight over to the fire, he licked his finger and touched each of his men on the forehead.

'I know if any of you have been bought by the Government while I have been away this saliva will boil on your heads and burn you to the brain,' he said. 'There is nothing like that, Muthee,' (muthee meaning elder) assured Wambararia respectfully.

Kimathi walked round the fireplace to get on the windward side where the smoke would not bother him, ordered one of his men to move out of his way, then sat down and gazed at the burning logs and sticks.

'We have looked far for you,' said Wambararia. 'We were wondering whether we would ever see you again.'

'You look far, Wambararia, only when you have no food left,' replied Kimathi.

The tone of his voice was soft, so Wambararia knew his brother was not really angry, and he tried to argue the point.

'We also have been without food since yesterday, but we have still been searching for you.'

'Speak the truth!' Kimathi retorted. His voice this time was louder, and it was plain that Wambararia had started something he would regret. He had roused

Kimathi by answering back. He had put himself in the dock, and would have to find his own way out.

'That is the truth, Muthee,' pleaded Wambararia. 'And Ngai knows it because he brought us together again. We went all the way to Karia-ini, then down through——'

'Shut up, you bastard,' interrupted Kimathi in English. With that he leant forward and picked up one of the burning sticks of bamboo from the fire. Holding it in both hands he probed in the ashes and scraped out a bit of scorched bone which he must have seen when he sat down, a bit of bone which his men had thrown into the fire after they had chewed the meat off it.

'What is this?' he asked, looking at Wambararia and tapping the bone with the tip of his stick.

When it was obvious that Kimathi had found him out, Wambararia turned cold with fright and begged his brother to forgive him. The bone, he said, was the only food they had eaten. But his pleas made no impression on Kimathi, who, without saying another word, stretched across and thrust the red hot end of the stick into his face. Wambararia's cheek and lips were burnt, and hot embers fell into his skin jacket.

'*Niahera, niahera*,' chimed the others, meaning that he had been sufficiently punished. After that nobody said another word. While Kimathi slept peacefully that night, his men remained on guard round about him, listening to the noises in the forest, thankful that their leader had been found.

The next morning after the dew had dried on the grass, he was led by Wambararia to the rest of his gang. It was not until the evening of the 23rd of April, the day we abandoned our fruitless search for him in the Mwathe region to the west, that he summoned Jeriko to give him a full account of the Itha river battle. The names of those of our men who had been identified were recorded in his little red diary, and he ordered his henchmen to kill them whenever they were seen again 'before one is given time to blink'. Then prayers were said throughout the night, and Ngai was thanked many times for having kept Kimathi from accompanying Jeriko on that fateful day.

The next morning, after Jeriko had gone away out of sight and earshot, he had the men brought before him, one at a time. He questioned each one closely, and accused them of being traitors. We soon discovered that this was typical of Kimathi, who invariably suspected there was a spy in his camp when his gang suffered casualties.

During the questioning he discovered that some of the men had come upon elephant tracks during their flight towards Kimathi's hide-out and, to hide traces of their own tracks, had stepped inside the hard, dry prints of the elephants. When Kimathi heard this he was horrified. He was sure it was an omen of ill-fortune to tread on the tracks of elephants. In a fit of anger he ordered all the honey in the camp to be brought and sprinkled on the feet of those who had used the elephant trail. Only this would appease the evil spirits. Then he chased everyone away and sat down alone to study a tattered and soiled copy of *Napoleon's Book of Charms* in which he had implicit faith. There he worked out what to do next. He decided he had to move quickly to a new area.

It was the 5th of May before we were ready to launch our next operation against Kimathi. Once again we used two teams of eleven men, but on this occasion we armed them to the teeth and replaced those who had been compromised with others who had not. For several days we concentrated on the Kahare-ini sector and on the forest areas between the Itha and Muringato rivers. We found the hide-out he had been in when Jeriko's party were encountered, and the traces of honey spilt on to the ground when those who had followed the elephant trail were cleansed.

What a difference there was between this hide-out and one of Kimathi's I had seen in the Zaina valley in August 1953! That one had been a most elaborate affair. It consisted of seven bamboo huts; two of them were almost ten feet square and the rest half this size. There were doors in all four walls of each hut to allow for a speedy getaway. The roofs were rainproof. The walls were windproof, and in his own particular hut he had a bed, a table, several log stools and a mosquito net, which he sat under when he had his meals so that the horse flies would not bother him.

Though the old site had been some distance from the nearest river, he had laid on adequate supplies of water. From a spring seventy yards uphill, he ran a chain of hollowed-out bamboo poles down to one of the huts. All day and all night fresh water trickled down the pipe. There was a large food store neatly constructed of smooth river stones, manhandled up from the river bed. In this he kept his meat cold and fresh and safe from rats and other forest scavengers which would easily bite a way through timber. None of the huts was used by his men. The other large one was a meeting hall, used only when other terrorist leaders visited him; three of the small ones were cooking houses, one for the cooking of his own food, one for the food of all the young women he had round him, and one for the food of a witch-doctor he had with him in those days, a little man named Wangombe Ruga, who, when his own predictions clashed with Kimathi's dreams, surrendered to save his skin. Then there was the hut for the water, and finally a pit latrine, erected not for purposes of hygiene, but to prevent hyenas howling round his camp, as they are attracted by the smell of human excreta. All his guards lived in little shelters, built in a circle round him, but these were placed well away from his central apartments. They did not enter without invitation.

The hide-out Kimathi had been sitting in when Jeriko's men brought him the news of the Itha river battle, however, consisted of literally nothing but a few square yards of cleared bush, where grass had been cut and laid for him and his men to sleep on. There was no bed, no stools, no cooking hut, no food store, no water point. His only protection from the weather consisted of a few thin bamboo sticks stuck in the ground at both ends and covered with a waterbuck skin.

We went back to Jeriko's hide-out, which was very similar, in the hope that some of the gang might have returned to look for the documents Thurura had tried to swallow, but the absence of tracks showed that nobody had been there since our team pulled Thurura from the thornbush and carried him away.

About a mile north-west of this hide-out, however, we found a broken and bloodstained stretcher. It was made of two long poles interlaced with bamboo and tied with muondwe bark, and had obviously been discarded when one of the poles had snapped. It was right in the middle of the area where the running gun-fight had taken place, and our men were surprised that they had not seen it before. A little further on they found traces of more dried blood, now nearly washed away by the rain. They found more blood on some large water-lily leaves near a stream, and it looked as if these leaves had been used to wipe the wound of an injured terrorist. We realized then that Thurura had not been the only casualty among Jeriko's party.

It was common knowledge in the forest that Kimathi

would never allow his movements to be hampered by a
wounded man, so we began a careful search of the banks
of the stream. It was obvious that the terrorist must have
been very badly wounded to need a stretcher, and when
it had broken there was every likelihood that he had been
left near water, as Kimathi's gangsters had more than
once before put badly wounded terrorists beside water to
die or recover. But despite all efforts the search was
unproductive, and we were back to where we had
started.

Then only three days before the operation was due to
end, the pendulum of fortune swung in our favour.
Several miles inside the forest, one of the teams discovered
a recently set game snare, and four men were left to
ambush it, while the balance moved over the crest of a
little hill to lie in wait. That evening, as the ambushers
lay silently beside the trap, they heard the bushes rustling as though a small group of men was forcing its way
through. When our men first heard the noise they knew
it was Mau Mau, for every few moments the rustling
stopped and there was silence. This was normal terrorist
practice. They were listening for danger. The noise came
closer and closer, the pauses grew longer and longer.
Finally, from where they were lying, our men could see
the upper branches of the bushes shaking. Out stepped
two of Kimathi's men, who crouched down to peer under
the foliage at their trap which was no more than thirty
feet away.

'It has not sprung. Let us go on,' one whispered, and
on they cautiously went, passing within arm's reach of
one of our men lying in ambush.

Seconds later both had reached their trap. They
touched the trip-stick, and the powerful pliant pole
sprang up with great force. As one set to work on the buck
path, removing fallen leaves and twigs, the other thrust

the trap forks deeper into the ground and sharpened the ends of the trip-stick so that it would give at the faintest touch. Then they took hold of the pole and began to bend it back the reverse way to give it greater elasticity At that moment our men jumped up, their guns ready. The trappers realized they could not escape. One raised his hands high above his head in surrender, while the other let go of the pole and sat down on the ground, saying, '*Wooi, wooi*, don't kill me. Don't shoot!' They were handcuffed together. Their trapping exploit was over.

These were the exact circumstances for which we had prayed. This was the type of quiet operation, the 'snatch', which would bring Kimathi's men secretly into our hands. We learnt all about Kimathi's recent behaviour. Shaking with fright, the two trappers, Kinanda and Ngomari, told their story so fast that they hardly paused for breath. Some days after the fight at the Itha river, after Kimathi had poured the honey on the feet of his followers and studied his *Napoleon's Book of Charms*, he split his force of forty-nine terrorists into six separate mbutu or sub-gangs to reduce tracks, for he was certain that Thurura would give the Government much information and that a major operation would result. According to Kinanda he had then set off northwards towards the Amboni river with fifteen men and Wanjiru, his woman; Wambararia, his brother, had moved off with four others in another mbutu; Jeriko had gone away with six; Nyoka with six; Juma Abdalla with eight, and Wamuthandi with four.

Before these mbutu went their various ways, Kimathi told them not to leave the Tree Tops Salient, and he ordered the leaders to send word when the area was safe for him to return, but he warned them not to do this until sufficient time had passed to make it improbable that any operation would be mounted on Thurura's information. He was to be sent this news by way of a certain mururua or cape chestnut tree which everyone in his gang knew. This tree would be his posta (letter box). In one of the dark hollows of its trunk the letter for him was to be left.

The two trappers described how they had been in Nyoka's mbutu only one day when Nyoka had decided to go on a long safari to Wuthering Heights, in the northern Aberdares, where game could be trapped more easily, and where there would be plenty of honey now that the rains were over. They had pleaded with him to allow them to stay in the Tree Tops Salient, for if Kimathi were to hear that every man in the mbutu had gone to Wuthering Heights he would punish them severely. Nyoka had seen reason in this and agreed to their request.

They had, therefore, been left on their own while Nyoka went north, and they did not know where any other members of the gang had gone. The news was gratifying, as we realized that we could keep our two prisoners for quite a long time before the gang suspected that they had been captured. We soon made a new plan. One of them was to write a letter to Kimathi and we would place it in the mururua letter box. The letter would tell him to return to a certain bomb crater which he knew well. It would tell him that the Tree Tops Salient was now safe. It would tell him that there had been no pseudo-gangs or Security Forces in the forest for some days. But it would not tell him that we were going to be waiting at the bomb crater when he came.

Before the team and their two prisoners finally withdrew from the forest, Kinanda took them to the terrorist who had been carried on the stretcher. After the pole had broken this unfortunate individual was carried to the water's edge where his wound had been washed with the lily leaves we found. Then some thick green leaves were stuffed into his wound to check the bleeding, and after being given some water, he was left to his fate. For three nights he lay there, constantly bathing his head with the cold stream water to cool his hot body, then, feeling a little stronger, he had dragged himself downstream in the water for nearly a mile before crawling up the bank into the forest where he collapsed. Sick, hungry and in great pain, he had lain there throughout the night beating off packs of hyenas and screaming wildly every time the beasts came close to him. Kinanda had heard the screaming, and had asked Nyoka if he could go to the aid of the man, but Nyoka had refused this because Security Forces might be waiting nearby. It was not till Nyoka left for Wuthering Heights two days later that he and Ngomari crept up to the place. The wounded terrorist was still alive. His feet had been so badly bitten by cane rats that most of the flesh round his ankles was gnawed away, and his white ankle bones were protruding from the flesh. His stomach was grotesquely swollen and bubbles of blood oozed from his wound whenever he moved. His whole body was caked with blood and earth. In a faint, barely audible whisper, he told Kinanda and Ngomari his story. And they listened to every word with care, for they knew he would die, and by the custom of the forest it was very important to hear the last words of a dying man. Then, when he had finished, he raised his head a little off the ground and, speaking a little louder, said to Kinanda: 'Kill me because of the pain. Do not leave without killing me.' And Kinanda obeyed, cutting off his head with one swift sweep of his simi. That night the hyenas howled louder than ever, and Kinanda remembered a saying his old father had once told him:

Nyota wa gikuo ndunyotokagwo.
'Death's thirst is never quenched.'

Chapter Twelve

A SERIES OF MISHAPS

Njira ndiraga mugendi 'Huruka'

The road never says to the traveller:
'Take a rest.'

THE days ahead were frustrating in the extreme. We searched in vain all over the Kimathi area. We looked on every hill and on every ridge, in every valley and in every ravine, but the answer was always the same.

We had already posted Kinanda's letter in the muru-rua tree, but Kimathi had not come to collect it. Far north in the Wuthering Heights region more teams searched for Nyoka in the hope that he might know where Kimathi had gone, but again we had no luck.

To add to our miseries, two of our collaborators were killed by a wild buffalo. Our team was moving through the forest when there was a sudden, violent commotion immediately in front of them. Some days before a large buffalo bull had been caught in a Mau Mau snare made of six strands of barbed wire rolled together, tied firmly at one end to a heavy stump and looped at the other so as to fit over the animal's massive head and horns as it came along the path. The bull had dragged the stump many miles through the forest until it was exhausted. The barbs had made deep cuts in its neck, much flesh had been torn away, and its forequarters were covered in blood.

A buffalo is a dangerous beast at the best of times, but this bull had been maddened by pain. It had not noticed the approach of the team until they were almost upon it. Then it erupted with a volcanic lunge of fury. Its horns tore savagely at the earth. Branches and bushes were flung high in the air.

Our men fled to the nearest tree, but the trap wires had snapped, and as they ran the buffalo swept down on them. In a matter of seconds the first victim had been trampled down and gored. A moment later the bull thrust its horns into the chest of a second man and shook the life from his body. Then the bull was off, crashing into the forest. Its victims were a mangled, bleeding mess. Nothing could be done for them. They were both dead.

When the news of this tragedy reached me late that afternoon, I set off at once, with the remainder of the team, to shoot the beast. A buffalo in this condition could be a serious menace to our men. The heaviest rifle we possessed was a service .303, which was by no means an ideal weapon for the job, but we had nothing else. First we went back to the spot where the buffalo had last been seen. There we examined the broken strands of wire on the tree stump and the mutilated bodies of our two terrorists. It looked as if every bone in their bodies had been broken. The spine of one of them had been smashed in several places, for though he was lying face down on the ground, his buttocks and legs were folded back over his head and shoulders.

After dragging the corpses to the foot of a large tree, we set off in search of their killer. At least there was no difficulty in following the buffalo's tracks. Buckets of blood were splattered about. The bull had, in fact, bled so profusely that the trail was a continuous red stream. We had only been gone about twenty minutes when we saw it. Part of its back was just visible over the top of the grass. It lay still. As soon as we saw this we stopped, half expecting it to rise, but there was not a twitch from it.

Very slowly I edged my way round the side until I could see the back of its neck, and from there I found I was also able to make out the outline of its chest. For some time I stood there to see whether there was any sign of life, but still there was no movement. To make sure, I put a shot through the back of its neck before walking forward. The loop of barbed wire was still round its neck. With that last fatal plunge the barbs had cut the buffalo's jugular vein and it bled to death.

Two days later another team came on a rhino in one of those areas of the Tree Tops Salient where it is foolish to walk unless you carry a reasonably heavy rifle. For two hundred yards there was not a tree at hand, only thick matted bushes through which they could not see and could not run.

They were almost in the middle of this patch when the rhino charged and, realizing that they could not run fast enough, our men dropped to the ground. As the rhino dashed through them with its horn just above the ground, it stepped squarely on one man's leg, breaking it like a twig, and ripping a huge piece of flesh from his thigh.

When the rhino made its first charge, all but the injured man scrambled away to safety. He had to watch the animal come crashing through the bush towards him again, but this time it charged through a collection of skin bags which had been dropped by the others. It carried two or three of these on its horn for some yards before slinging them into the air. Then the rhino disappeared for good.

As I was talking to a terrorist after this incident, I mentioned that all we could do was hope that the rhino and buffalo were giving Kimathi an equally tiresome time. 'No, Kinyanjui,' he said, in all seriousness. 'I think Kimathi has given them the Mau Mau oath.' This was the sort of thing the Mau Mau thought Kimathi could do.

Then one of our teams operating high on the Moorlands of the Aberdares was surprised to find, as they were slowly climbing a ridge late one evening, that a gang of terrorists were singing to them from the crest of an adjoining ridge a few hundred yards away to their left. When they stopped to listen, the singing also stopped. When they moved on, the singing started again. Then one of the singers shouted across the valley to tell our team that if any of our men walked towards them they would all run away.

Bewildered by this odd encounter, our team moved on up the ridge. This time they walked more slowly in order that they could hear what the gang was saying. Much to their annoyance the songs were insulting. They were being called 'women' and 'thirsty goats' and 'porcupines'. Our men were so annoyed by the abuse that they decided to go after the singers, but when they reached the crest of the other ridge there was no one left. We were worried when we heard about this, as we naturally suspected that the role of our collaborators had become known, and that the Mau Mau had embarked upon a campaign of ridicule. But in the weeks which followed we found nothing to confirm our fears, for the same team had many excellent successes. The riddle was not solved until months later when we captured the entire gang of a Mau Mau general named Kimbo Mutuku, who said that he and his men had been responsible. They had thought that our men were part of Kimathi's gang, and as Kimbo hated Kimathi for having thrown him out of the higher councils of the Mau Mau years before and sent him into exile for gaining too much popularity, he had tried to get one back on Kimathi.

Gethieya and I shared the general depression. Once we had to spend two days and two nights without food, blankets or shelter at the highest point of the Aberdares, where the altitude is just short of 13,000 feet. Our clothes were soaking wet, we could not light a fire because there was no firewood, and it rained without stopping. Our spirits were so low that we found we could not even talk to one another.

Our tempers were not improved when, after long and tiring journeys through the forest, we sometimes found that our rations, which had been hidden away at pre-arranged rendezvous, had been completely devoured by hyenas. Their powerful jaws and sharp teeth ripped open tins of corned beef and fruit without difficulty, and all we would find they had left for us were a few scattered and torn pieces of tin. Sugar, tea, aspirin and paper bags were their favourite foods, but on one occasion they ate a thick tarpaulin sheet used to cover the rations. One particularly hungry hyena chewed up my fountain pen and a torch.

We weren't always unlucky. After one trip, when we had been taking food out to some of our men, we made a detour through the forest to the scene of a Harvard aircraft crash, as we knew that the terrorists obtained much of their trapping wire from crashed aircraft. After climbing all over the fuselage for several minutes, we returned to Nyeri, where we learned that months before a military unit had booby-trapped the wreckage with twelve two-inch mortar bombs and eight hand grenades.

And sometimes we laughed. Once Mac nearly lost his trousers to an inquisitive baboon who picked them up, studied them for a few minutes, and then threw them down in disgust. Then Mac discovered a chameleon while we were camping on the Moorlands, and proudly walked back among the bivouacs of the terrorists to show them his find. He did not realize that there is no reptile which the Kikuyu fear as much as a chameleon, which they think is made by the devil. When the terrorists saw it on his arm they rushed into the forest, and we had to spend many hours persuading them to return to the camp. Sometimes we were confronted with certain rather boisterous terrorists who considered themselves a little too clever. We put them in the back of a Land Rover and placed a small dried turtle I had bought years before in Las Palmas on the floorboards beside them. Nothing could have deflated them better! They were so terrified of the turtle, the likes of which they had never seen or heard of before, that they struggled desperately to squeeze through the hatch behind the driver's seat, while everyone who was in the know roared with laughter outside. When they realized that they had made fools of themselves they became far more placid.

While walking one day towards a place on the Moorlands not far from the old Fort Jerusalem track, where I was to hide some rations for a team, I came over the crest of a small hill to find several eland staring intently in the direction of a patch of scrub on the far side of a ravine. Realizing that they had been alerted by some unfriendly visitor, I stopped to study the scrub carefully with binoculars for some minutes but, as I couldn't see anyone, I guessed that they had probably been frightened by a leopard.

Having buried the rations in a thicket and carefully erased my tracks, I set off back to my Land Rover which I had left two miles away. I had gone about a mile through the forest fringing the Moorlands when, much to my surprise, I came upon a party of native forestry workers who had been sent up to repair a broken log bridge on the Fort Jerusalem track. They were quite unaware that an operation was in progress, and were relieved to hear that I would take them down the mountain in my Land Rover.

Three days later I was back at the food point with Gethieya for the rendezvous. The team of seven were there waiting for us with four additional terrorists whom they had captured, but their tempers were strained, for they had come to the food point to collect their rations on the day I had brought them, but they had found nothing there. They had been without anything to eat for six days. Remembering the forestry workers, I immediately suspected that some of them had gone back up the mountain and stolen the food, whereupon Gethieya and I located and questioned every one of them. They denied everything. A week later the riddle was solved—seventy miles away on the edge of the Fort Hall reserve, where a friend of mine called Ian Pritchard was operating his pseudo-gangs caught a small group of terrorists led by a notorious gangster named Noru Makinya. Noru and party had feasted for a week on our rations. As a rule Mau Mau regarded any place visited by Security Forces as highly dangerous, so I journeyed to Fort Hall to hear what Noru had to say about it. It turned out that he had been in the patch of scrub when I had come over the crest of the hill, and he, in fact, had attracted the elands' attention. He had watched me closely as I hid the rations, then, when I had gone, he crept over with his men to see what I had buried. He pelted the spot with stones for some minutes to make sure it was not a booby-trap, then he had dug up everything and gone away.

It was not until the 4th of June that we made contact with Kimathi's gang again, and then we did so only because some of his men made the grave mistake of going into the farming country after a rainstorm to steal potatoes, which made concealment of their tracks on the return journey impossible.

We had always been on the alert for reports of produce-stealing along the eastern side of the Aberdares bordering

on the Kimathi area, so that when one morning a wireless message was passed to us in the forest giving the
location of the theft we were quickly off the mark.

During the night a gang had crept down to a farm
near the Nyeri polo ground and dug up a large quantity
of potatoes. In the potato field the terrorists had been
both wise and careless. After digging down and removing
the potatoes from the plants, they had carefully replaced
the earth in the hope that no one would notice until the
plants began to wither some days later. But in the darkness they had not realized that the earth they replaced
beneath the plants was the earth they had dug up with
the potatoes, which was much drier earth than the earth
on the surface. The result of their mistake was fatal, for
early the following morning when the native gardeners
went to the fields to work, they immediately noticed the
different coloured patches of earth and began digging to
find out what had happened.

The footprints of the gang were plainly visible in the
neat rows of potatoes and, within a few minutes of their
arrival, our team had discovered where the gang had
posted their look-outs and where they had regrouped
before setting off with their spoils for the forest. Instead
of making straight for the edge of the forest two miles
away, the culprits had first gone in the opposite direction towards a large labour camp which they circled
before zig-zagging back. They had set a false trail so that
the blame would fall on native labour. But our terrorists
had themselves done the same thing countless times before, and no time was lost in picking up their tracks on
the forest edge.

Inside the jungle the tracks were more difficult to
follow as the drippings from the trees had smudged the
marks, but despite this the team were close on their
quarry by late evening. As darkness fell they fanned out

and combed through the undergrowth in a long line. They were now nearly ten miles from the point where the gang had entered the forest.

They had almost decided that it would be best to call off the hunt until daylight again when a strong whiff of smoke drifted over towards them. They all smelt it.

Without a word they crawled upwind on their stomachs. In a few moments they could see the faint glimmer of a light from a shielded fire against the leaves of the trees. They crept on until they could hear voices. Then they stopped and waited in silence while two men went forward to reconnoitre, easing their bare feet forward inch by inch, probing with their toes in case there was a dry branch on their path which would crack. When the shrill call of forest hyrax pierced the silence of the night, they bounded forward, for nothing could be heard above this.

The two scouts came right up to the edge of the hide-out and peered through the bushes at five terrorists sitting round the fire. A large cooking-pot supported by three sticks was boiling away, and they could hear the water bubbling as the potatoes cooked. They recognized every member of the gang, which was led by Wambararia, Kimathi's brother. He was one, they thought, who must not get away. Our men could hear every word that was spoken. The gangsters were discussing the night's raid, saying that they would never go near the labour camp again because many dogs had barked. One of them was very annoyed with the water carrier because of the dirty water he had fetched from the river, but the others joined in and said that the whole river had been fouled by elephants drinking higher up, and that there was no cleaner water anywhere in the area.

The scouts studied the scene for several minutes, hoping to see where the gang's guns were stacked, but without success. Probably, they thought, Kimathi had kept them all. Then, as silently as they had come, they retraced their steps.

As the pot was being lifted from the fire, the gang was rushed from two sides. The terrorist who was holding the pot dropped it, spilling the boiling water and hot potatoes over one of his equally startled companions. Another reeled back shouting, 'It is us, Kimathi, it is only us.' He was soon disillusioned. Wambararia was cool and collected. He quickly grabbed a satchel of documents lying on the ground beside him and threw it into the fire. He was hit on the head with the butt of a revolver when he tried to stop one of our men snatching it back from the flames.

When all five of Kimathi's men had been handcuffed together, the fire was stoked up and, in the flickering light, the documents were studied by the only man in our team who could read. While this was happening Kimathi's men saw their valuable potatoes being eaten with relish by their captors, who did not save them one. Then the fire was beaten out, and the party set off to a place called Muti uri Cieni, or the tree on the vlei, where I was to rendezvous with them next morning.

It was nearly eight o'clock before I arrived at Muti uri Cieni, and as I came in sight of the tree I saw the team jumping up and down and chatting excitedly about something which was obviously amusing them a great deal. But Wambararia and his companions, who were still handcuffed together, were sullen and unamused.

'*Kai ni atia?*' ('What is it?') I asked.

'What we have seen today is the best,' replied one, and told me what had happened. After the prisoners had been handcuffed together, the party had travelled several miles through the dark forest towards Muti uri Cieni before they had come upon a good place to sleep. Before daybreak they were on the move again, and were just getting to the tree where we now stood when a rhino had charged, scattering everyone. Two of our men had seen the manacled quintet making good speed across the clearing towards a spinney of trees. To stop any escape attempt, they had chased after Kimathi's men without worrying unduly about the rhino, which was still charging to and fro round the tree.

As the terrorists were about to reach the spinney the rhino apparently caught their scent and came racing over after them, but veered off into the forest before reaching them. The departure of the rhino was seen by all our men, but not by the terrorists. There was panic in the spinney. As the fastest of the five, Wambararia dashed into the lead and dragged the others along behind him. But when he reached the nearest tree and started to climb it, he was pulled down by one of his companions who, standing firmly on his back, tried to get up the tree himself, but he too was pulled down. Sure that nobody was going to climb that tree, the group picked themselves off the ground and headed for another, but they did not all aim at the same one. All pulled in different directions, swearing and cursing at one another. When pulling seemed futile, Wambararia tried pushing, but this too got him nowhere. In the end the gang collapsed in a tangle. All the time our team were rolling over and over in the grass at what they still claim was the funniest sight they have ever seen.

Wambararia looked like Kimathi, although he was far shorter and stouter than his brother. He had scars on his cheeks and lips where his brother had burnt him that night after the Itha river battle. Once back in camp he became the centre of attraction, and all our terrorists huddled inquisitively round him. He seemed suspiciously voluble and soon announced his readiness to lead us back to a place where, he claimed, his brother was hiding. Within an hour we were on the move again with Wambararia at the head of a specially selected force. But perhaps he was telling the truth for, after all, if anyone should know Kimathi's secrets, it should surely be his brother, and Wambararia's scars showed that he had reason enough for revenge. We decided to attack as soon as the hide-out was pointed out to us.

We might have guessed what the outcome would be. Instead of leading us directly to his brother, Wambararia marched us straight across the front of the hide-out to expose us, then, as if he were still not sure that the gang had gone, round in a circle and back to it through an area of extremely thick, dry bamboo, where a noiseless approach was impossible. When we reached the deserted hide-out and realized what had happened, he said he hoped we would kill him. At least he was a faithful and loyal brother!

Everything in the hide-out, such as cooking pots, meat, trapping wires and other valuables, had been left behind, which showed how quickly the gang had left. Two days later Wambararia told us how he had deliberately exposed us. We also discovered from him that Kinanda and Ngomari, the two trappers we had captured, were not the lone terrorists from Nyoka's mbutu they had claimed to be. They had belonged to Kimathi's personal mbutu, and had known exactly where Kimathi was at the time of their capture. They had, in fact, just come from him, and would have gone straight back to him if they had not been caught. The story they told us about the Mururua letter box had been invented on the spur of the moment.

We learnt all this because Wambararia would not believe that he had been tracked to the spot where we caught him. Instead he was convinced that either

KINAINI BASE CAMP FROM WHERE THE FINAL OPERATION
AGAINST KIMATHI WAS MOUNTED

A LOOK-OUT POINT IN THE MATHAKWA-INI AREA WITH
PSEUDO-TERRORIST KEEPING A WATERING PLACE UNDER
OBSERVATION

ONE OF OUR TEAMS ON OPERATIONS. TEAM LEADER ON THE RIGHT, WEARING WATCH, WAS TAUGHT TO READ THE TIME TO BE PUNCTUAL AT RENDEZVOUS

INSPECTOR RICHARD MACLACHLAN (MAC), BETTER KNOWN TO THE PSEUDO-TERRORISTS AS 'CHARUBU' (MOUSTACHE)

Kinanda or Ngomari, or both, had put us on to him. Not
long before both of them had been with him in a hide-
out nearby, and had heard him speak well of the area
and say he would go back to it. Sure that they had done
him down, he decided to expose them as much as he
could, and he told us about their ruse. This set off a
chain reaction. Infuriated by Wambararia's revelations
and accusation, both Ngomari and Kinanda then told us
all they knew about Kimathi and his brother, and they
told us much. This episode of betrayal and counter-
betrayal broke all resistance among the rest of Kimathi's
men in our hands, but ill-feeling ran so high that we had
to hand Wambararia over to the regular police to avoid
trouble in camp.

Now Kimathi was really on the run. Throughout the
emergency he had never experienced such a series of
narrow shaves. It was all too much for his nerves. He
called on Ngai more than he had ever done before. He
became so suspicious and highly-strung that the sight
of an old rusted bully-beef tin thrown away months before was enough to send him skittering sideways like a
shying horse. If an aeroplane flew overhead, he would
insist that he had been seen and move his camp without
delay. He would not touch a Government surrender
pamphlet for fear that it was poisoned, or in case it had
some curse on it, which, in his own words, 'would burn
out the eyes'; the print of an army jungle boot in the
forest would send him dashing off into another area,
and the print of a bare foot found in a place which he
knew none of his men had visited or passed through
was enough to send him off on a lengthy journey.

Among Wambararia's documents was a letter Kimathi had written to him some days before, describing a
dream in which Ngai had spoken to him:

F

As I was sleeping I felt someone hold my hand. I woke up and heard God say to me, 'My son, come with me.' I stood up, and Ngai took me by my right hand and we walked through a most beautiful forest where there were many red and yellow flowers and big birds with green wings. There were also many big rocks out of which clean springs were flowing. And Ngai took me to a mugumo tree [wild fig] which was bigger and higher than all the other wild fig trees in the forest, a tree that was like a father of all trees. And I rested my hand upon it. When I did that, Ngai spoke to me again and said, 'This is my house in this forest, and here I will guard you.' Then the tree came up out of the ground and went up into the clouds and I did not see it again. Then it rained very hard and I woke up a second time, but I could not remember where I had seen the tree. But from this I know that the house of Ngai is in this forest and it must be found and from now onwards no person shall pass a mugumo tree without praying, otherwise he will anger Ngai and be destroyed.

As a result of this dream Kimathi began a series of pilgrimages to certain parts of the eastern Aberdares where large wild fig trees were growing.

Chapter Thirteen

TECHNIQUE PERFECTED

Kuri arume na maiuria ndua

Some are males and some can
only fill the gourds

or

As sheep come to the fold,
some are good and some are bad.

WHILE a select group of the very best of our converted
terrorists was searching for Kimathi in the Tree Tops
Salient and the Mwathe, the rest of the force was not idle.
They too had been formed into gangs and went back into
the forest to work for us. By the end of June we had over
ninety hard-core Mau Mau operating in the Aberdares
on our side, and success bred success. A hostile gang
fighting against us yesterday became a tamed gang
fighting for us today. We were not exactly converting
these desperate men, but we were certainly recruiting
them.

No Mau Mau could merge with the Kimathi gang,
but our technique of penetrating and living in with other
Mau Mau gangs proved immensely successful. Time after
time our collaborators contacted gangs and merged with
them without difficulty. Every meeting was celebrated
in great fashion with much praying and smearing of
smelly animal fat on everyone's forehead to wash away
any impure thoughts that might have entered their
minds during the time that they had been apart from

one another. Everyone would then retire to some secluded part of the jungle where all the available food was eaten.

When the gang fell asleep their guests would lie down with them and pretend to sleep also. Sometimes friend and foe would lie beneath the same skin cover, their bodies close together for warmth. But as the night wore on, as their hosts snored and sighed and turned, our men would be waiting for the signal to strike. Sometimes someone in the gang would be restless, and the time for action had to be postponed. So as to warn the leader not to rise, cautionary coughs would echo round the hide-out, and all would be silent for another hour or so. But when the moment finally came, the job would be done with the utmost efficiency. The Mau Mau would wake to find that they were being tied by the feet or covered by armed men who were no longer friendly. Every week an average of twenty-two terrorists were accounted for in the forests by our teams using this technique.

Normally it was only when a gang had posted armed sentries round its hide-out that anyone was killed, and these were invariably the sentries themselves. This suited us well, for in order to make progress we had to have information, and only live terrorists could supply this. When a team was preparing to capture their sleeping hosts, some of them would sneak away to deal with the sentries. Sometimes they found them leaning against trees blissfully unaware of their danger. These we were able to overpower without noise or resistance; sometimes we found them alert. They would challenge our men and we would have to have a good excuse for not being asleep. The excuse our men usually gave was that they were going to relieve themselves. Normally our men walked quite boldly up to the sentries, whose positions had been carefully noted beforehand, and as they went they would stretch their arms back and yawn as though they had just risen from a deep sleep. They would whisper to the sentries about the coldness of the night, about the noise of an animal or about a pain in their stomachs. They would watch their man until he relaxed, then, with the speed of a wild cat, they would drop him and hold him down. Any resistance meant death. Nothing but imme-diate submission was good enough, for they knew their adversaries, they knew it was a matter of life or death. Mau Mau were not people to take chances with! It was like holding down a leopard—give it a chance to free a foot and you could be clawed to death. But not once throughout these operations did anyone escape.

Sometimes the terrorists asleep in their hide-outs were remarkably slow in coming to their senses. It always amazed me how tense and sensitive a Mau Mau gang would be when no sentries were guarding them, and yet how utterly oblivious to danger they would become when sentries were posted. One night when a terrorist named Kabangi was captured, all the sentries round about and all his companions in the hide-out had been securely tied up before he awoke. He had been asleep on the ground with six others, all closely packed together and covered with a single dirty piece of hessian, when our team struck. Four men on his left and two on his right had been pulled to their feet and handcuffed before he stirred. But even then he did not wake up. When one of our men grabbed his hair and shook his head, he turned over onto his side and mumbled, 'What are you doing? Do you think I am a woman?' With that he went to sleep again.

Another, named Kaburei, who was captured with three others, complained bitterly to his captors when they tried to shake him awake that he was far too tired to visit the traps. After his ankles had been tied together with rope and he had been pulled to his feet, his first exclamation was, 'I seem to feel that I am dreaming of being tied up!'

But these were certainly exceptions. In most cases our teams had to act quickly and decisively, sometimes before they were ready. The Mau Mau practice of lying packed together like kernels on a corn cob sometimes made it very difficult for a team leader to extricate himself without waking the gang up. There were cases where sentries screamed out and woke the whole gang. There were even cases where the gang never went to sleep at all.

For months the sole preoccupation of all these terrorists had been mere survival. They lived like animals. They survived because of their animal skills, and when caught they reacted like trapped animals.

I often saw terrorists a few moments after their capture. Some would be standing there wide-eyed, completely speechless and shivering violently from shock and cold. They would think of the moment of death, and that moment seemed very near. Others would be past the stage of thinking at all. Mad with shock, they would shout and struggle or froth at the mouth and bite at the earth.

Under these circumstances it was not easy to remember that they were fanatics who had enjoyed killing children and slitting open the stomachs of pregnant women. They were savage, vicious, unpredictable as a rabid dog, but because they were now trapped, muzzled, powerless, and terrified, one felt like giving them a reassuring pat.

Those who were suspected of committing specific atrocities or major crimes were handed over to the authorities with the least possible delay to stand trial; those against whom no definite charge could be made, but who were, nevertheless, particularly bad characters, were sent off to detention. Some, we felt, would respond to civilization fairly quickly, others might take longer, others would probably never respond. They would remain a menace to society as long as they lived.

But there were some not directly linked to serious acts of terrorism. There were terrorists who, though still hard-core Mau Mau, possessed information which would be of great value to us, and seemed prepared to give it to us. We kept these and recruited them into our force. I talked to them, Gati talked to them, other members of our teams talked to them, and soon they were ready to go back into the jungle to hunt for others. And so the snowball rolled.

The selection of bad from worse, useful from useless, co-operative from stubborn, was always done with care, and required a sound knowledge of the psychology of the Mau Mau on the one hand, and of the Kikuyu people on the other. Above all else, those selected had to be the types who would respond to our efforts to win their unstinted allegiance. We were trying to persuade them to change their regiment; not their souls. To them I was probably a rival and more powerful gang leader. I did not represent good as opposed to evil, but I did represent hope for them and their tribe. It was a tricky business. You could never be really sure that the man you had chosen to go back into the forest with you would not cut your throat when your back was turned. All you could guard against was going back into the forest with someone who would definitely cut your throat at the first opportunity. Fortunately, our judgment proved to be reliable, for, of the hundreds of Mau Mau whom we captured and used again in the forest, there was not a single case of desertion or loss of firearms.

The Mau Mau in the forests never had the remotest idea of what was going on. But it was not very long before the stage was reached when more than half the Mau Mau gangs on the Aberdares were actively working for us against their own leaders and against their own organization. Sometimes a considerable number of our converted gangs happened to be out of operations at the same time and came into contact with one another. Their surprise was understandable. 'Since when have you been doing this job?' 'How did you get here?' they would ask each other. Naturally as more and more changed side from the forest to our force, the task of recruitment and indoctrination became easier. Force of numbers became the key to their conversion. It was a far cry from the day when Gati and Hungu first met us on the Fort Jerusalem track. But Gati was still our principal aide. He was the regimental sergeant major of this force as well as an operational leader. He was responsible for discipline, and meted out the punishments such as cooking, fatigues and load carrying.

The task of keeping every man in our force recognizably active, that is to say acceptable to the remnant hostile gangs as comrades-in-arms, was extraordinary difficult, and as much work and time had to be devoted to this extremely important aspect of our technique as was devoted to the actual hunting of Mau Mau. We had to get all our teams seen in the forest from time to time; we had to get their members to write letters and keep up the chain of correspondence in the jungle; we had to keep their food stores going. You could not remove half the Mau Mau from the forest and expect the subsequent absence of hide-outs, letters, traps and the many other signs of Mau Mau activity to pass unnoticed by the other half. Often we were able to arrange meetings in the forest where our teams would confer with hostile Mau Mau. Having proved their loyalty to the cause and extracted all the information they possibly could without giving the game away, our men would withdraw with their tongues in their cheeks and the way would be paved for more operations. Only Kimathi and his bodyguard still remained beyond our reach. They were a completely different problem. They were too cunning, too careful, too suspicious and too isolated to fall to the ruses which brought the others tumbling down.

As a result of all this, our knowledge of the forest and of those in it increased steadily, until we found we were able to predict gang movements with a surprisingly high degree of accuracy—except for Kimathi. Every terrorist who remained at large was known personally to most of the men in our teams. It would be quite wrong to say that this admirable denouement was the result of our efficient leadership. Far from it. The brains behind the whole show were the converted Mau Mau themselves. They were undoing the bolts in the evil Mau Mau machine which they had themselves constructed. They knew where the nuts were, and they had the tools to do the job.

While we were confident, therefore, that we had the forests well in hand, and were rapidly getting rid of their occupants, the elements of Mau Mau still active outside the forest in the native reserves and the farming lands were being whittled down by the Kenya police, the Field Intelligence Officers and their pseudo-gangs, the Tribal Police Reserve, and the Kikuyu, Embu and Meru guard. These forces gained such a firm grip on their areas that if a terrorist were to flee from the forest, he had little hope of survival. It was a case of jumping from the frying pan into the fire. It was not only in the forests that new techniques had been developed. The reserve or settled area terrorists, the Mau Mau oddments who lived in holes beneath the ground like rabbits and came out only in the dead of night to steal food—they were far more difficult to find than you might think, and it took much skill to root them out. They did not live in holes you could see. Their underground hide-outs, or dakki, were

F*

elaborately built, and you could sit on top of them, or even build a house on top of them, without knowing they were there. In most cases the only tell-tale sign of a Mau Mau dakki was a hole in the ground about the size of a penny, through which they sucked air. They had a method of kuhitha muromo or concealing the entrance from inside which was almost as perfect as the forest Mau Mau's method of kuhitha makinya or concealing the tracks. Finding them in the darkness of night while they were out foraging was next to impossible; finding them in their holes by day was hardly any easier. Yet with the combined effort of the Security Forces, backed by the District Administration, a remarkable method of ferreting out these dakkis and tracing their occupants was discovered. It is a story which emphasizes, amongst other things, the great part which the Kikuyu people themselves played in the latter part of the emergency to rid their home areas of Mau Mau. In the same way as they had started the evil, they were now putting an end to it. Outside the forest the Kikuyu loyalists were the people of whom the Mau Mau were the most terrified; inside it was again the Kikuyu who were finally cutting out the cancer.

Needless to say, this was a time when the eyebrows of all connected with operational Intelligence were kept perpetually raised by a flow of conflicting rumours and reports. The great tribal conspiracy of silence based on the Mau Mau oath had been broken by the imminent defeat of the terrorists. Hundreds of Kikuyu now tried to ingratiate themselves with the authorities by passing information to Government officers in the field. A great deal of this information was false. Where it concerned the movements or activities of terrorists cut off in the jungle, few were able to assess its reliability. Almost daily we received reports pin-pointing certain gangs in a given area. Almost daily we knew, but could not reveal, that the gang was working for us and was anything up to a hundred miles away. Yet there was nothing particular to be alarmed about in this trend. It was one of the many peculiar manifestations of a peculiar cause.

It had always been an odd sort of war, and the case of Thiongo was by no means untypical. Quite early during the emergency Thiongo had been severely wounded in the thigh when his gang was ambushed while stealing food in the reserve. He had dragged himself several miles into the forest, and for fourteen days had lain without food or water, unable to move from the spot where he had finally collapsed. On the fourteenth day, when his strength was almost exhausted, he saw a small monkey peering at him from the branches of a nearby tree. Then the little creature came down in hesitating jerks, until it was only a few feet away. Something was attracting it. When the monkey came close to him he tried to catch it, but it quickly darted up a tree. Throughout the day, for some reason, the monkey refused to leave the area. Instead it kept on sneaking back to the place where Thiongo was lying, and eventually he was able to grab it by the tail. With his last ounce of energy he strangled it and ate its raw, warm flesh. This gave him a new lease of life, for three days later he was picked up unconscious but alive by a passing gang, with bits of monkey meat and skin still beside him. He was taken away up the mountain where he eventually recovered. The gangster who found him and revived him was Gati. Months later Gati, who had now joined us, caught Thiongo, who in his turn became a team leader. In five months he accounted for forty-seven other terrorists. Yes, it was a peculiar war!

Thiongo and his fellows had learnt what was harmful and what was not, what would kill and what would nourish. They had been forced to adopt a way of life which even the most primitive of pastoral African tribes could not match. The Masai bushmen, the Wanderobo hunters and other primitive African tribesmen, who had gained a reputation for their skill in tracking and hunting, were beginners by comparison with the forest terrorists still at large in 1956. It was odd that people of this calibre should become the main arm of the Security Forces. It was odd that the elimination of the last die-hard remnants of Mau Mau should depend, not on the arts of modern warfare, or upon the ingenuity and strength of civilized man, but upon an abnormal and primitive skill practised by an abnormal and primitive people.

Chapter Fourteen

THE CATTLE RUSTLERS

Ruri kuma njora, ruticokaga tuhu

A knife which has been unsheathed does
not return into its sheath without having
done some work.

BEFORE we got rid of Wambararia he told us something
of his brother's future plans. Kimathi was certain that all
the setbacks and alarms he had suffered in the previous
two months were attributable to a curse. This could only
be removed by making a sacrifice, and he had told his
men of his intention to do this at the next full moon. He
also told them that after the ceremony had been held, a
big feast was to take place, and that everyone should
save meat and honey for it.

We had only known this for four days when we
received a report that a number of valuable cattle had
been stolen by a large Mau Mau gang from a cattle pen
on a farm near Mweiga. Naturally we thought that
Kimathi was responsible, and that the raid had been
carried out in order to get plenty of meat for the feast.
The fact that Mweiga touched the part of the forest in
which Kimathi was living made us feel sure that we were
right.

The raid had taken place during the night, and had
been discovered by a Mkamba herds-boy, who, on going
to the pen to let out the cattle, had found some of the
animals missing, others straying and the door broken

down. The police found, from the hoof-prints, that the stolen animals had been driven away at a cracking pace towards the northern end of the Kimathi area. They signalled this information to us, and we rushed a well-armed team to the edge of the forest to pick up the trail.

The exact time of the raid was not known, but as Mau Mau seldom stole cattle before everyone was asleep, it was almost certain that it had occurred after midnight. But the gang could not have reached the forest edge before daybreak if the raid had taken place after three o'clock, so it must have been between midnight and 3 a.m. that the cattle were driven off.

The speed with which terrorists drove stolen stock through dense forest always surprised us, and we learnt that it was never safe to estimate this at less than an average of six miles an hour. It was now nine o'clock in the morning, and assuming that the raiders had not stolen the cattle until three o'clock, it was clear that they had a possible start on us of thirty-six miles. There was clearly not much point in following the tracks from the forest edge. Instead, we took the nearest track up the mountain, and dropped our team off about fifteen miles inside the forest, so that they could work their way along the slope, parallel to the forest edge, until they intercepted the spoor.

Despite our first belief that Kimathi was responsible, we soon had our doubts. Thurura and Kinanda, both former members of his gang, told us that over a year before Kimathi had put a stop to stock thieving because nothing betrayed a gang's position more easily than the hoof-prints of stolen animals. But who else would dare to venture into Kimathi's forbidden territory?

Our team had not been gone many hours before they came to a steep ridge down which the raiders had tried to drive the cattle. Here they had obviously had a great deal of trouble with the animals as it was clear, from the spoor, that the cattle had refused to bound down the ridge and, instead, had scattered in two directions, leaving behind a trail of churned-up earth where their hooves had cut through the blanket of forest mulch and raked up the dark brown soil beneath.

Gati, the leader, had no difficulty at all in following the tracks, and made good speed with the team. At places along the winding trail through the forest, his men found long, broken sticks which the terrorists had used to beat the cattle. For a considerable distance the raiders had driven the animals along well-defined game tracks, but then they turned off and plunged straight through the thick forest. Every few hundred yards the team would pause to listen for the sound of the animals crashing through the undergrowth, but they heard nothing and realized that they were still a long way behind.

After a few miles, however, the team came to a really formidable hill. The raiders had driven the beasts straight up the steepest parts towards the top of the Aberdares; and, in order to travel fast, had seized hold of the animals by their tails. They had knotted the cows' tails, as you would knot a piece of rope. As the knot tightened with the weight of the terrorists hanging on behind, the agonized animals had threshed along faster and faster, pulling the raiders up behind them.

Without the benefit of a similar ride up the steep hills, our team fell far behind. On and on they plodded, breathless, sweating, aching, but determined. They could not keep it up, however, and as the sun fell behind the jagged edge of the Simbara Range, throwing a gigantic evening shadow over the whole eastern side of the mountain, the track faded until the team was forced to stop.

They had not been resting for long when they heard something coming up the hill towards them along the same route they and the raiders had already taken. As the sound came nearer they could hear that it was a man panting from the steep climb, and Gati quickly hid his men on both sides of the track to wait for this newcomer. Then three of Kimathi's men appeared, climbing breathlessly up the hill towards them. On and on they came until they were right in the middle of the ambushers. Then the team pounced, threw them to the ground, tied them up and began to question them about the cattle raiders.

The story the prisoners gave was an odd one. They said that they had been with Kimathi a few hours before when they had heard the cattle raiders passing through the forest. They described how Kimathi made everyone stand in silence for some minutes while he climbed a tree where he listened to the animals lowing and to the thuds of the sticks as the raiders beat them along. Then he had climbed down and told his men that he thought our troops were driving the animals along in the hope that the Mau Mau, in their hunger for good red meat, would follow them up to collect any left-overs—and walk into a trap. But to make sure he had detailed three of his men to reconnoitre while he vanished in the opposite direction. Although this story turned out to be right, it did not ring true at the time. Our men could not understand why, if Kimathi had been close enough to hear the cattle lowing, his scouts should now be so far behind the raiders. Knowing how expert Kimathi's men were in setting false trails, they were inclined to believe that the thief was Kimathi himself, and that the three prisoners had only lagged behind because there had not been enough tails to pull every member of the gang up the steep hills. Our men took the prisoners a short distance away to spend the night under guard, while the rest of our team lay down to rest and plan the pursuit which would begin when the first calls of the partridges were heard in the morning.

As our men sat resting in the last moments of daylight, they talked quietly about the country. Far down, probably forty miles as the crow flies, they could see the flickering lights of the little railway station of Naromoru, then further south they could barely make out the cluster of buildings of the Police Training School at Kiganjo. There, they thought, was a world so different in every way, a world where people wore clean clothes, where there were cars and lorries, and bugle calls, and where there were such things as windows, roads, corrugated iron roofs and even bicycles. All these things frightened them, for the thought of civilization now seemed foreign and dangerous and made them shudder. They felt they could not speak about the gadgets and complications of the world outside without feeling chilled and worried. But nearer to hand, inside the forest, there were things they understood well, things which comforted them. Just behind them was Mutanga Riua hill, where, according to legend, an old Kikuyu had once taken off his githii or skin-coat and hung it over the sun, and that was why the Aberdares was always a cold and misty place. Then, on their left, was the 'muirigo wa Mwathe' or Mwathe ridge, along which the Mau Mau had passed in their thousands during 1953 and 1954 on their way to Deighton Downs, Ndaragwa and Ol Kalou, and still further to the left and slight lower down was the part of the forest they called Gitara-ini, named after the gitara in which Kimathi used to perch to shoot elephant. They remembered the .450 elephant gun he used to have, and wondered what had become of it, and they remarked on how clever he was in being able to kill an elephant with one shot! They also remembered how the terrorists used to rush up to the dead elephant as soon as one fell to hack off the meat before the troops could hear the shot and come up, and how Kimathi used to send large gangs through the forest to kill porcupine because they ate the ivory taken from his elephants, precious ivory which he boasted he could exchange for aeroplanes! All these things they could talk about freely, for they were a part of their lives.

They were too high up the mountain to hear the familiar noises of the jungle. It was even too cold for the hyrax, for the ngaiyaga or bush baby and even for the hyenas. As these were the noisiest of the jungle creatures at night, there was an eerie quietness about the place.

Suddenly the quiet was broken by the lowing of cattle. It was the sound of an animal in agony—the long, drawn-out, guttural noise that is made when a sharp knife is slicing through a cow's neck, a familiar noise as this was the way the Kikuyu slaughtered their animals. The sound was clear and loud, and came from the far side of the ridge.

Instinctively every man rose. Those with guns pulled their magazine pouches outside their skin jackets because in the darkness there was no purpose in concealing them; those with simis lifted the straps of their sheaths over their heads to prevent them from catching on dry branches when they moved through the forest. In a long line they went down the valley and up the ridge on the far side, halting every few minutes when the cattle lowed, to check their course. Only three men were left behind to guard the prisoners. All the rest were on the move. Less than an hour had passed before they saw a large fire burning in the centre of a patch of bamboo, low down in a valley where the land was shaped like a saucer. Only from the high surrounding ground was this fire visible. They stopped and watched for some minutes, and could see much darting to and fro in front of the flames. Down there the cattle were still lowing intermittently, and the noise was echoing against the hillsides.

Quietly they moved down, first threading a course through a belt of black forest, and then through bamboo, where it was too thick for a sentry to see any distance. As no sentry would stand where he could not see, they knew that their route of approach was secure.

The last two hundred yards was covered by very thick bamboo, through which they had to crawl on their hands and knees, but here, as the bamboo was young and soft, they were able to push ahead without making a noise. The glow of the fire became brighter and brighter as they crept nearer, and at last they could see everything clearly from the fringe of the bamboo. The spectacle made even our hardened terrorists shudder.

Before them was an oval-shaped clearing covered with a low grass. In the middle of this arena a large fire was burning furiously, throwing up a spray of bright red sparks. Three or four terrorists were standing round it, branches in their hands, beating out the flames whenever they began to spread over the surrounding carpet of grass. All round this area were groups of terrorists, some skinning dead cattle, some keeping live beasts at bay, others slaughtering the animals. The scene was a whirl of moving figures.

One of the terrorists would hold a cow by the tail while the others hacked at its legs with their simis until all four legs were cut right off or were hanging by no more than a shred of skin. There the cow would be left, struggling hopelessly, unable to move except by rolling from side to side, and the group would pass on to another animal and start all over again. While this was happening a different group was making its rounds. They would grasp the cows' heads firmly, then twist them violently and lay them on the ground. While some held it down, others would cut the jugular vein and collect the warm blood as it squirted out. When all the blood had been drained off, they would move on to another animal, leaving the cow in its death throes. Finally another group would come up to skin the carcass and carve up the meat.

This blood-bath continued deep into the night. As each carcass was carved up the meat was carried out of the arena a few hundred yards into the bamboo forest where, towards midnight, three small fires were lit, and some of the raiders began roasting the choicer pieces of beef. The smell of roasting meat drifted over to our men, who knew that all would not be quiet until the terrorists had fed. This would take some time, as each man would eat five or six pounds of meat, if not more, and drink the blood drained from the animals' throats.

By this time our team had identified the gang, and realized that Kimathi and his men were not involved. It was the gang of a notorious terrorist named Ndungu Gicheru, whose cattle-rustling exploits throughout the emergency had cost the farmers of the Central Province many thousands of pounds. Our men knew that they could merge with Ndungu's gang in normal times without any difficulty, but these were not normal times. If they were suddenly to walk out of the bamboo where they were lying, they would either send the forty raiders running into the forest, or start a battle which might be costly. They decided to wait until the gang had left the arena and huddled round the three fires. Then, with luck, they should be able to creep up and attack at close range.

When all the cattle were dead and their moans had ceased, the voices of the raiders were clearer. Someone, probably Ndungu, was telling those sitting round the fires that nobody should roast meat as it was important to get away from the area as soon as possible, in case the large fire in the arena had been seen from the hilltops.

This advice was rejected by the majority, who were only interested in the meat. After all, they said, no Security Forces would come at that time of the night, and it would be quite safe to sleep there until dawn.

At exactly 4.15 a.m. by Gati's watch, when the fires were smouldering and the raiders were asleep, our team crawled forward towards the three cooking points, which were only a few yards apart. As they slid forward they could see the dark shapes of the sleeping raiders, who were huddled together on the ground by the hot coals. They could see one sentry silhouetted against the skyline, but our men were not worried, for in a large gang like this there were bound to be people getting up and down throughout the night and this would serve as a useful cover for their own movements.

The silence was broken by the loud clatter of machine-gun fire. All three fires were sprayed simultaneously from a range of about ten yards. As red-hot cinders flew up and danced crazily above the ground, the raiders began to stir. Some got up and ran into the forest, some stood up only to fall back and roll over on the ground. Some did not move at all. Then the firing stopped, and our men heard the moans of the dying lying round the fires, then the night was silent once again.

That night Ndungu Gicheru lost nearly half his gang, and he himself, his leg broken by a bullet, could only crawl a few hundred yards away. There he had spent what was left of the night in agony. When he was found at dawn, he was sitting with one leg outstretched and the other, which was almost severed below the knee, tucked lifelessly under him. Ndungu had suffered just as the cattle had suffered. The mills of God grind slowly, but they grind exceeding small.

Chapter Fifteen

KIMATHI'S PRAYER TREES

Gutiri muthenya ukeaga ta ungi

No day dawns like another.

THE July mists now rolled down over the Aberdares, turning the beautiful mountain into a gloomy, damp and depressing place where the sun would not be visible for several days at a time. The birds didn't sing and the bees didn't buzz. When the July mists come, all the sounds of the forest which are stimulated by warmth cease abruptly, as though the needle had suddenly been lifted from Nature's gramophone.

In the early days of the emergency a dramatic rise was always expected in the number of terrorists surrendering towards the end of July, for the cold, dreary mists drilled through their resistance. But those days had gone. The gangsters who still held out had long passed the stage when discomfort could make any impression upon them.

Yet, just as the long rains brought about a change in their mode of living, so did the mists. The valleys, the open grasslands and all places near cold running streams were abandoned in favour of the thicker parts of the jungle where the undergrowth provided a little warmth. There was a tendency to leave the higher ground and come lower down the mountain; and there was always a drift towards the bamboo belt where easy-burning firewood could be found.

As far as we were concerned, there was no better time for our operations. We were able to move about the forest far more freely without being seen and we could get up far closer to the gangs undetected. As soon as the mists arrived, therefore, we redoubled our efforts and instead of sending two teams against Kimathi as we had done in the past, we now turned out in force to hunt him down.

On the 2nd of July, no less than seven strong teams were bowled into the Tree Tops Salient. They went in from all sides—from the top of the National Park track, from the Kinaini river, from Ngoju-ini, from Kihuyo in the east, from Muti uri Cieni in the north and from the Ruhotie valley in the north-west. Their whole effort was to be concentrated in the bamboo belt.

Results followed quickly. On the 4th of July, a particularly misty day, five members of Kimathi's gang were captured and a further two were killed when one of our teams encountered the gang west of the Kinaini river. The groups did not see each other until they were a few yards apart. By a stroke of luck all Kimathi's firepower had been travelling with him in the rear, and our men were able to open fire on a largely unarmed vanguard which suffered heavily. The gang had only been licking its wounds for twenty-four hours when we were at them again. Guided by one of the prisoners taken in the first encounter, we caught two more of Kimathi's men at a game trap the following day and overpowered them without loss to ourselves. This was something of a landmark as it was the first time that any of Kimathi's gang had guided us on an operation without attempting to mislead us.

Morale amongst our men soared with these successes. To brush with the gang twice in such a short space of time was remarkable, and to have done so without losing any men was miraculous. The hunt went on with a fresh zest and our luck still held good. Eighteen days later, on the 22nd of July, Juma Abdalla, one of Kimathi's sub-leaders, fell into our hands during a night raid and soon after that we scored the greatest success since the fall of Wambararia. Jeriko and all but two of his mbutu were accounted for in a very spirited fight which cost us two of our collaborators.

Kimathi and some of his men had camped within a stone's throw of Jeriko, whom we had last seen at the Itha river. To all intents and purposes, there were two separate groups living near one another. Why Kimathi had chosen to do this we could never find out. It was quite unlike him to depart from his usual defensive tactics of sleeping in the middle of his men, who would spread themselves round him over a wide area. Unfortunately, the tracks which our teams had followed led them to the wrong group and they went into the attack not knowing that the balance of the gang was close at hand. No sooner had they rushed Jeriko's hide-out than they were fired on from behind, and this cross-fire killed two of our men. As before, as soon as the battle was joined, Kimathi departed like a scalded cat. As always, he somehow managed to escape when he should have been caught. But his gang of fifty men was now reduced to a total of twenty-one men and Wanjiru, the woman. We were halfway to our goal. But there was another set of figures which interested us even more. Just before the Itha river engagement, the gang held, according to Thurura, exactly 2,011 rounds of ammunition. Jeriko told us that they were now down to 246 rounds and in this last battle they had used forty or fifty rounds. The gang was losing its punch.

No one was more surprised at the way we were whittling down the gang than Thurura. A day or so after Jeriko had been caught, I turned to him and asked,

'Wasn't it you who said that capturing Kimathi's men was impossible?' '*Noguo*, Kinyanjui,' he replied, 'but I also warned you that Kimathi would be the last man in the forest to be caught and you will see if I am not right.'

After this last operation we withdrew from the forest for some days to interrogate the new batch of prisoners, and during this period, which carried us out of the mists into the sun again, we were able to review all the facts at our disposal and plan anew.

It was during this period that we suddenly realized we already held a vital clue to unravelling Kimathi's future plans. The clue was his dream—the dream about his god, Ngai, taking him by the hand to the mugumo tree —the dream he had written about to his brother. With mounting interest we listened as Jeriko and his friends told us how Kimathi would walk every week to certain parts of the forest where large mugumo trees were growing. There he would stand with his arms raised above his head, his forehead pressed against the tree, praying aloud to Ngai and pleading with his god to return and save him. We were told that these pilgrimages were the very breath of life to him. He believed that if he did not make these pilgrimages Ngai would not only let him die but would also destroy his ngumo ya njamba or fame of warriorship. Kimathi now believed that prayer would bring him immortality and, just as important to him at the moment, an immortal reputation.

On hearing about this we jumped for joy. Here, at last, we had advance information about places in the forest which Kimathi would visit—and visit come fire or come hail. How easy it would be! No longer, we thought, would we search laboriously through the jungle for his tracks, game snares, hide-outs and food stores. Instead, we would watch the mugumo trees like hungry vultures and take him by surprise when he came to pray. But Jeriko had not finished, and his next words threw a less encouraging light on things. He told us that Kimathi would never visit one of his trees without first sending his men to search the area and make sure that no enemies were about. Then, even if their report was favourable, he would not approach a tree until he had circled it twice. The first time he would be anything up to a mile away, the second time closer in. During these circuits he would move as quietly as a leopard, studying the forest with extreme care and thoroughness for traces of human tracks. If he found any, even if they were days old, or even if he found marks which he could not identify, he would bound away like a frightened buck. Knowing his unusual instinct and powers of self-preservation, we knew how difficult it was going to be for us to ambush these trees.

Yet there was more to it than that. We were told that there were at least forty such mugumo trees in the Kimathi area and he was liable to visit any one of them. Sometimes he would go to one particular tree three times in succession, then, after his third visit, he would stay away while his most trusted lieutenants would return to see if any Security Forces or pseudo-gangs had passed by. If they had, he would assume that there was a traitor in his camp and, in Jeriko's words, 'the case would crack a log'.

Nevertheless, we were making progress. It would certainly be easier to watch the trees than work almost blindly in those hundreds of square miles of forest. The rains and the mists had passed and with them had gone the days when the gangs crouched and huddled in their hide-outs, which were comparatively easy to find. Now they would have unwound again and be roaming the length and breadth of their private domain. Kimathi and his men could be anywhere in either the Tree Tops

Salient or the Mwathe. But apart from the considerable problem of actually getting to the trees, we now had great difficulty in persuading our men to go there. They found the thought of ambushing Kimathi at his 'places of prayer' most disconcerting. 'What would Ngai do,' they asked, 'if he found his chosen altar desecrated?' Though they did not altogether believe Kimathi's dream, they did not disbelieve it either. After all, they knew that he had dreamt before of Security Forces arriving at a certain place at a certain time; and these dreams had proved to be correct. If he now dreamt that Ngai would return to one of these trees, who were they to dispute the prediction? Perhaps some evil spirit did haunt the trees. Perhaps it would jump down and kill them as they lay beneath the branches.

Fear of 'Ngai's altars' became so deep-seated within the next few days that at odd intervals during the nights at camp, one terrorist after another would sneak away alone to some dark corner where, facing Mount Kenya, he would pray to 'Ngai' to save him. The drop in morale became so serious that all prayer or talk of 'evil spirits' had to be forbidden. And with our men in this edgy, erratic state, we were quite unable to start on offensive operations again. All the curious thoughts disturbing their minds had to be neutralized. But we had to step lightly, for here we were dealing with a potent and deep-rooted part of all African life—fear of evil spirits.

While these troubles were upon us, Kimathi was facing an identical problem with his gang. Our men were frightened of the mugumo trees and wanted to have nothing to do with them; his were frightened of the mugumo trees too. After the many setbacks they had suffered, his followers began to wonder whether his habit of praying beneath the trees was the cause of their misfortunes. Before Kimathi began these pilgrimages, they had been so lucky. Had Ngai, they wondered, deserted their leader?

Three or four times Kimathi called his followers round him and held all-night sessions where he would read from his Bible and warm them with the fire of his oratory. Once again he poured out the mixture of parable, proverb, mythology and venom which had once swayed thousands of forest men. Now the last handful gazed wide-eyed and bewildered as he spoke. All the time he was trying to convince them that their only hope of survival lay in prayer beneath the mugumo trees.

We soon heard about these sessions and sensed that Kimathi was beginning to panic. He seemed to have lost all stability of mind. Instead of eating the precious honey which his followers found in the forest, he made them mix it with earth and animal blood. After this mixture had been put on the ground in its container, it would be covered with green leaves and herbs while hymns were sung. Then, after some of the contents had been sprinkled on the ground round the hide-out to act as a spiritual 'fence' for keeping out evil spirits, he would take the rest away to a mugumo tree as an offering to Ngai. All eyes had to be averted as it was poured over the roots at the foot of the arboreal altar.

Among the many things his gang had stolen in early raids were a Bush wireless set, a porcelain washing basin, an assortment of silver knives, forks and spoons and a large bathroom mirror. All these things were now condemned as 'unclean'. They were collected and hidden away in a cave where we soon found them. Those men who had carried the goods to the cave were forbidden to eat or touch food for three days on their return and were made to wash their hands in the blood of a buck taken from his traps. Sometimes Kimathi's travels took him across the rough forest roads. He invariably insisted that all those who crossed the roads should wash their feet in the first stream they came to because 'after the enemies' vehicles had driven over the roads, they would be poisoned like the fangs of a puff adder'.

Twice he journeyed to Karia-ini, a point high on the Aberdares where, in 1953, a large bamboo shelter had been constructed by the Mau Mau for their meetings. At this shelter, which they called Karuri Ngamne Head-quarters, he had once met all the leaders of his various 'armies' in the days when Mau Mau was at the height of its power and he was the supreme commander.

All that was now left of the building were a few ant-eaten and weather-worn poles, two or three twisted roof beams and several rows of log benches where the leaders had once sat. This had been the home of Mau Mau's highest councils, now there was nothing but decay. But Kimathi rose above his surroundings. He walked jauntily up the aisle between the rows of empty, dilapidated benches just as he had done long ago. With revolver in his hand, he stood looking down on an imaginary audience. Raising his voice, he would call the 'meeting' to prayer and order everyone to stand up while he delivered his sermon. He would remind his listeners that Ngai had made Gikuyu, a man, and Mumbi, a woman, the Adam and Eve of the Kikuyu, and placed them at the top of Mount Kenya where, in time, they had given birth to nine daughters. From these the nine clans of the tribe had sprung. He would say that in the same way as Ngai had sent Gikuyu and Mumbi to the snow-capped peak, he had only chosen those with the 'thickest blood' to enter the forest. In this way Ngai had separated the corn from the cob so that the worthless members of the tribe could be annihilated and so that the traitors in the tribe could be washed away by blood falling from their own bodies. Ngai had a very large black book in which the names of all those who died in the forest would be recorded. They alone would find a new, rich, beautiful land in a different world to which Ngai would take them.

While his guards stood round about he would go on speaking for hours, allowing his imagination and his memories free play in his mind. Sometimes, he would raise his arms as though he were trying to silence a jubilant, cheering crowd. Now and then he would pause and, pointing to an empty bench, he would call upon the leader of the Mburu Ngebo Army of the Rift Valley to speak, for that was where its leader had sat in bygone councils. He would call upon other leaders of other 'armies' to speak. In his imagination, he would listen to reports from the leaders of Ituma Demi, Mei Mathathi, Gikuyu Inoro, Mburu Ngebo, Ruheni, Kimuri, Kareba and other defunct Mau Mau 'armies'. As he stood silently with his head bowed, he heard the still voices of his men who had died. These lonely council meetings would give Kimathi new strength. For days after his visits to Karuri Ngamne he would be in better heart, giving new inspiration to his followers and showing a more tolerant attitude towards his fellow men.

To him these imaginary meetings were not old memories revived. They were a reality. He believed he had actually seen his ghost audiences. He believed he had heard each of his old-time leaders speak out. He often brought up the subject later with his men and asked them whether they did not agree that such and such a dead leader had spoken very well and was a fine warrior. But the gang never questioned his sanity. After all, if the great Kimathi had heard the dead speak, who were they to disbelieve him? Had he not been blessed by his dying grandmother and chosen to lead the people? The frets and fears of his followers centred on one thing and one thing only—his visits to mugumo trees. These pilgrimages were something completely new, something never seen or done before by the Mau Mau, and the Mau Mau were always suspicious of anything which had no precedent.

When we learnt about these odd events we were sure that Kimathi was going mad. Some of our collaborators who knew him well said that if we kept up the pressure much longer, he would probably kill Wanjiru and then shoot himself. This was our greatest worry, for if he just disappeared the myth of his omnipotence would survive in the forest. It was imperative that we should find him before he chose suicide.

Just before we began operations again, another incident shook Kimathi's gang, and we soon heard about it. One day towards the end of July, Kimathi's only surviving woman, Wanjiru, the Mau Mau queen whom all men served, the woman who had never collected wood or cooked food in the forest, suddenly became the centre of a row which resulted in the death of two of Kimathi's men.

With a dirty buckskin coat over her shoulders, Wanjiru left the hide-out and walked a short way into the forest to relieve herself. Kimathi had suddenly become aware of her absence and lost his temper, because he had not been told of her departure. The longer he waited for her to come back, the more furious he became. When Wanjiru finally did appear, walking back towards the hide-out with two of his men, he lost every vestige of control. He imagined that the two men had lured his woman away to seduce her. Without a single word, he walked over towards them and shot them both with his revolver. Then he grabbed Wanjiru by the wrist, stripped the coat off her shoulders and for almost an hour beat her naked body with stinging nettles. Then he ordered his terrified followers to bury the dead and move on to a new hide-out in case the shooting had been heard.

That night Wanjiru was very ill. She developed a severe rash, while her body was badly blistered and bruised. She cried repeatedly for water but Kimathi paid no attention to her nor would he allow anyone else to go near her. When he had fallen asleep, one of his minor leaders named Wamuthandi, who had been upset by Wanjiru's moans, slipped quietly away with four friends and went down to the river to fetch water for her to drink and they took two rifles with them. Having drawn the water and climbed back up the hill, they came in sight of the hide-out where, to their horror, they saw Kimathi standing up and asking where they had gone to. As they stood there listening, they heard him tell another terrorist named Wanyee to collect ten men together and go to arrest them. They heard Kimathi say that they were to be brought back with their hands tied as he proposed 'to grind them like corn in a mill'.

Wamuthandi and his companions knew they would die if they were caught, so that night they fled to the Marishimiti gorge nearly fifty miles away on the western side of the mountain, where they stayed until they were captured. Wanyee's ten men searched for the deserters for twelve hours, determined to kill them if they came across them, but they were unsuccessful. There is no doubt that Kimathi's men hunted for their ex-colleagues with enthusiasm and would have killed them with pleasure. Brother hunted brother, father hunted son and friend hunted friend. That was the Mau Mau creed.

Kimathi's own actions had now caused the death of another two and the desertion of another five of his dwindling force, leaving him with only fourteen men and Wanjiru. This was indeed a far cry from our first feeble efforts seven months before. Within a few days, two of the five deserters were captured by one of our teams and gave a vivid account of the cause of their flight from

DEEP INSIDE THE TREE TOPS SALIENT. THE NATIONAL PARK TRACK CAN BE SEEN ON THE RIGHT

A TEAM RESTING ON THE ROUTE TAKEN BY KIMATHI BESIDE THE MWATHE VALLEY IN THE LAST DAYS OF THE OPERATION WHEN HE WAS ALONE AND DESPERATE

DEDAN KIMATHI
LYING MANACLED
ON A STRETCHER
ON THE DAY OF
HIS CAPTURE

DEDAN KIMATHI

Camera Press

Kimathi. Their capture was a great help as those of our men who were still apprehensive about going to the mugumo trees became less frightened when they heard what had happened in the forest. It seemed that even Ngai was deserting Kimathi.

Chapter Sixteen

OPERATION 'WILD FIG'

Mutego ti ngoro, ni wathi warera

It is not the trap that counts,
but the art of trapping

or

A good archer is known by his aim,
not his arrows.

By the evening of the 8th of August, all the large mugumo trees in the 'Kimathi Area' had been plotted on our map. These trees are not common in the forest of the Aberdares, and they are quite rare in our hunting ground. Jeriko had said that there were at least forty, but we only found eighteen and ten of these were in spots which Kimathi would certainly not visit because the approaches were unsafe. We turned to the remaining eight.

That same night, eight well-armed teams made their way to the trees. The march was a taxing exercise in bushcraft. Our teams had to avoid open spaces where an alert sentry could see them; they had to avoid the likely resting places of bushbuck and duiker, for if Kimathi found the hoof-marks of a running antelope, he might suspect that his enemies were at hand; our men also had to avoid those birds or animals which raise an alarm as soon as they see human beings, such as the Sykes monkeys, whose loud warning calls can be heard for miles through the forest. Then there is the tiny little brown ndete or call bird. Whenever they see something move

they fly over and perch themselves on a nearby bush
where they jump frantically from branch to branch and
make as much noise as they can to tell the forest of their
discovery. He is a most difficult creature to get rid of.
Fortunately he chatters whenever he sees anything move
so he is a far less reliable 'alarm bell' than the less
excitable Sykes monkey and it can often be a pure waste
of time to check up on his warnings. But nothing was
ever too tiring or troublesome for the timid Kimathi.
Whenever he heard the ndete, he would study the situation from afar for some time in the hope of identifying
the cause of the bird's alarm, then, if he could not see
anything, he would dart away.

Some of the wild fig trees were several miles up the
slopes of the mountain and it was not until the afternoon
of the 9th of August that all our teams were finally in
position. In some cases the trees were growing in places
which were ideal for ambush, there would be adequate
cover for our men to hide themselves and good observation points at hand; but other trees were growing in
spots where a rabbit could not conceal itself, where the
trees had drained all the strength from the soil and not
even grass would now grow. Our men took up the best
positions they could find and after covering their legs
with their animal-skin coats to shield them from the
hard-biting horse flies, which can sting a man to the
border of frenzy, the long wait began. Here they were to
lie for four days and nights unless Kimathi favoured them
with a visit. Rain, heat, cold, wind, ants, caterpillars,
wild animals, snakes, and all the other dangers and discomforts of the forest would have to be endured as they
lay there. In those same positions the calls of nature
would be answered by turning slowly onto their backs
and scraping a small hole in the soft, forest soil with their
fingers. They would lie there as still as death, but all the

time they would be alert and sensitive for the faintest
rustle in the bushes, a suspicious sound or a movement in
the trees. The events of the last few weeks had not
lowered their respect for Kimathi's hitting power. They
knew he had many marksmen, excellent marksmen in his
ranks. They knew that two of his men had been gun-
bearers for professional hunters before the emergency
and could handle a gun as well as anyone.

I had often watched our teams on operations in the
forest. They would lie absolutely motionless for so long
that I wondered whether they would ever be able to
move their cramped limbs again. All the time their chins
would be resting on their clenched fists and they would
be staring at some particular spot where they believed
they would first see something coming. They were,
curiously enough, seldom wrong. Their stare would be so
intense you would think they had seen something and you
would try to see for yourself, but without looking at you
they would sense your curiosity and slowly shake a finger
to show there was nothing there. Sometimes you would
hear a rustle in the forest and look at them inquiringly,
but they would still be staring at the spot they had been
watching for hours. Perhaps they had not heard it, you
would think, but before you could move, they would
quietly whisper '*Ngima*' ('Sykes') or '*Thwara*' ('Buck')
or '*Kanyoni*' ('Bird') and you would lie back feeling
ignorant and a bit embarrassed. In the forest they knew
the answers to everything, outside to nothing. In the
forest it was always safest to leave everything to them.
After operating with them a few times you would very
quickly realize when something unusual was in the vicinity. Instinctively they would pull their fists away from
their chins and their heads would drop an inch or two.
This was a reflex action developed in the days when they
were often under fire. Then their heads would turn very

slowly in the direction from which they suspected the intruder was coming and by tapping a little twig on the ground or on a dry leaf, they would signal messages to one another. Their bodies would curl up. And then one man would give the signal to attack. A low in-drawn whistle meant 'Fire'; two sharp clicks with a finger meant 'Rush'; and when they fired, or when they rose to their feet and rushed, they would react with surprising speed, darting through the tangled, forbidding undergrowth with a grace and ease that were fascinating.

Often it would not be the recognized leader who gave the signal for action. The Mau Mau knew that in the forest it was the man who could see or hear best who was best able to direct the others, while the chosen leader might sometimes be unable to see what was going on.

We found that number 3 tree, which stood about a quarter of a mile south of the Itha stream, had been visited by Kimathi only two or three days before our arrival. Number 6 tree, about eleven miles to the west, had been visited two weeks before that. In each case there were traces of honey on the ground, honey which Kimathi had spilt there as an offering to Ngai and which had attracted a variety of butterflies.

The first day passed uneventfully, as did the second, although our team at number 2 tree heard a single rifle shot in the distance during the evening. But on the afternoon of the third day the monotony was broken by an incident which could have had far-reaching consequences. A strong wind blew up towards mid-day in the eastern sector of the Tree Tops Salient where number 1 team was operating. As the team lay bunched together beneath the tree, two large and very poisonous puff-adders fell from the branches on to the back of one of our men. Fortunately the reptiles wriggled off into the bush without striking at the petrified terrorist, but the team as a whole, was sure that 'it was an act of God' and that Ngai was angry with them for being there. They immediately left the tree and rushed back to our tactical base higher up in the forest. We did everything we could to convince them that the snakes had fallen out of the tree because they had been mating or because of the high wind. We told them that it was absurd to think that Ngai had thrown snakes at them, but they were still most upset. MacLachlan and I looked at my Arab-silver bracelet. Perhaps the evil spirits of the forest were going to defeat my lucky charm. Here was something which could alter the whole course of these operations and make our terrorists go on strike. Not even Gati, our formidable disciplinarian, would have been able to cope with evil spirits.

But the following morning, the fourth and last day of the operation, our patience was rewarded. At number 7 tree, which stood where the Mwathe and Tree Tops regions join, a single terrorist appeared for a moment some four hundred yards up the slope of a steep hill and quickly dropped out of sight. In that split second one of our men caught sight of him and signalled word to his companions. As this was the day when they were going to withdraw according to our plan, the team thought at first that a messenger was coming to them to tell them to remain where they were for another two or three days, but when the figure appeared again, closer this time, they were unable to identify him as one of our men. He was tall and heavily built, his hair, which was exceptionally long, fell over his shoulders and, unlike anyone in our force, he was wearing a shirt and trousers made of old tarpaulin.

The terrorist came lower and lower down the hill, jumping quickly from one thicket to another. At one moment our team thought that he looked like one of their colleagues named Thiaka. There was a whispered dis-

cussion. All were agreed that the intruder looked like
Thiaka but he did not move like Thiaka. Then about
one hundred and fifty yards away from the mugumo
tree, the intruder jumped into a particularly thick patch
of bush and did not come out again. Half an hour passed,
then an hour, then two hours, but there was no further
sign of him. It was all very odd. Our men were certain
that they would have seen him leave the patch if he had
done so.

When the sun was noon-high and their curiosity had
been stretched to its limit, the team decided to go and
look for themselves. Splitting up into two parties they
wriggled back on their stomachs until they were in a
small ditch from which they could circle round the flanks
of the hill, one party climbing it from the left and the
other from the right. Within five minutes they had regrouped and were searching together through the patch
of bush which the terrorist had entered. In the middle
they found another ditch about four feet deep running
along the hillside for nearly sixty yards. At its head and
also at a point where the mugumo tree could be most
easily seen, were the footprints of their man. They could
see where he had stood, not only on that day but also
several times before. The ground had been trodden hard
there and a light branch which had interfered with his
view had been snipped off with a sharp knife and tucked
away underneath the bushes to dry. Now it was obvious
that the intruder was one of Kimathi's men and that he
had been scouting to see whether it was safe for his leader
to come and pray beneath the tree.

Our men followed the tracks from the top of the ditch
to the bottom, where they disappeared into the forest.
There our men halted to discuss what they should do.
First they thought that it would be best to return to the
tree and wait until the scout had told Kimathi that it was

safe to come, but what if they had been seen? And then
they realized that they were supposed to withdraw that
same evening. Even if the scout had not seen them,
someone was sure to come out to look for them if they
did not go back to the base that night and there would
be a risk either of shooting their own friends in the darkness or of the searchers scaring Kimathi away. They
decided to follow up the tracks.

Gacheru was the most proficient tracker among them
and from the start he set a fast pace. Sometimes he
would stop for a few seconds to study some special mark
on the trail, but there were no real problems. The pursuit
went on from hill to hill, valley to valley, and river to
river, until Gacheru fell back to the rear and his place
at the front was taken by the next man. Like all good
trackers, Gacheru would get a bad headache after a few
miles. When you track human beings in the jungle you
do not focus your eyes on anything specific on the ground
but rather on the general scene ahead. In the words of a
most expert Mau Mau tracker, 'the ground is lifted and
brought up near the eyes so that the direction of travel
can be seen and not the footprints'.

The course taken by the lone terrorist led southwards
towards the bamboo in the massive Zaina valley, which
is almost two thousand feet deep in parts, and our team
was getting worried as tracking in bamboo is always difficult. Furthermore, as our men had no food left, there
was little hope of a meal for at least another two days if
they continued on their way. These thoughts were not
comforting, but the tracks were fresh, their blood was up,
and the team rushed on like a pack of hounds after a fox.

Throughout the afternoon the hunt continued. Fortunately the terrorist had swung westwards towards
higher ground instead of going down into the Zaina
valley and, as his course was fairly direct from this point,

it was clear that he knew exactly where he could rejoin his gang. But the pace of our team got slower and slower as the tracks became more difficult to see in the fading light. It was now a race against time, for once darkness fell the pursuit would have to be called off. Gacheru again took the lead and they moved on quickly.

They were beginning to wonder how far their quarry was going, for they had already tracked him some thirteen miles, when suddenly in the wind, Gacheru heard Kimathi's high-pitched voice. *'Wiyite Ritwa!'* (Name yourself!') Gacheru stopped. The team stopped with their weapons ready. 'Jeriko,' shouted back Gacheru, who knew that Kimathi could not have heard of Jeriko's capture, as nobody had escaped during the engagement. There was hardly a moment between Gacheru's answer and Kimathi's reply. 'Never,' he shouted, in English and with that pandemonium broke out in the bamboo about forty yards ahead as Kimathi and his gang dashed into the undergrowth.

Firing their guns from the hip, our team went crashing after them. They hurdled fallen bamboo poles. They climbed under others. And as they charged, they had to protect their eyes from the network of sharp dry sticks which are an added hazard to pursuit in the bamboo. The first of the running gangsters to come in sight was Karau, whom Kimathi had made a 'general' only a few days before. A burst of Patchett fire knocked a wooden honey container from his hand. He was not hit, but he lost his nerve and was found lying on his back with his knees drawn up to his chin as though trying to shield his heart from the next volley.

As the team paused to tie him up, a hand grenade exploded thirty yards to their left. Then there was a noise in another bamboo thicket just ahead. Three of our men opened up with their automatics. They were sure

G*

they had hit one of Kimathi's gang. Our men went forward. There was no sign that their bullets had found their target. As soon as they began to probe around, however, they came across a deep bomb crater covered with a tangled mass of bamboo. At the bottom was another of Kimathi's men. He had fallen into the crater as a buck would fall into a pit trap. The noise that our men had heard was caused by this man trying to climb out.

Immediately he saw the team on the edge of the crater looking down at him, the terrorist crouched in the shadows with his simi drawn ready to slash anyone who went down after him. He was told repeatedly that he was covered and should come out, but nothing would move him. Several shots were then fired into the crater but still he did not move or speak. Finally the covering mattress of bamboo was set alight and he was dragged out with a long pole as the flames licked about him.

Meanwhile Kimathi and his remnants were travelling fast. By the time Karau had been tied up and his companion pulled out of the crater, the gang had disappeared completely. In the last half-hour of daylight, there was nothing to be gained by following him as the hunt would have to be called off within a few minutes. So, taking a short cut through the forest and making the most of the dwindling light, our men and their prisoners set off at a brisk pace for base, which they reached just before midnight. All the way back they talked about Kimathi and his gang. Why, they asked, had Kimathi not been the one to fall into the crater? Karau told them that he had been to the ditch in the morning. He had been scouting for Kimathi just as they had guessed. What a pity, our men thought, that he had not been caught before he reached his leader, for then he might have led them even closer to Kimathi. These thoughts filled the team with anguish. But a cause of even greater anguish was

the fact that Wanjiru, a weak and powerless woman in
their eyes, had been with the gang and got away from
them. The disgrace of missing a mere woman was too
terrible to bear. They were sure that it would take the
ministrations of a medicine man and the sacrifice of a
black sheep to wash away their disgrace and stop their
comrades mocking them.

Their fears of being jeered at by their friends in camp
were, however, quite unfounded. That night when
Gacheru and his party arrived, everyone turned out to
hear what they had to say and when they heard that the
woman in question was none other than Wanjiru,
Kimathi's Wanjiru, they were not the least surprised.
Although she had been cared for like a child in the
forest, they knew that she could run like a gazelle, fight
like a cat, shoot like an archer and that she was more than
a match for any ordinary man. 'That one,' said Ruku to
Gacheru, 'that one is not a female. She is one to be
watched very carefully with two eyes in the front and two
in the back and never wag your tail when she is near.'

Later that night there was great rejoicing round the
camp fires. Gacheru and his team had much to say about
the day's events. As the flames from our eight fires
flickered against the trees, lighting up the ugly faces of
our collaborators, the story of the day was told over and
over again. Gacheru held the centre of the stage with his
stirring accounts of the pursuit and the battle. He stood
where all could see him demonstrate how he crouched to
peer through the forest when Kimathi had challenged
him, how he ran forward, and exactly what he had done
at the bomb crater. It was stirring stuff and the tale
of those miserable victims of the puff-adder episode
attracted little interest. The conversation went something
like this:

Ruku: 'Did you really hear Kimathi's voice?'

Gacheru: 'Very much so, like a horn being blown.'

Waira: 'Weeeee! At that time he was alert like a fly.'

Everyone: '*Noguo, noguo.*' (Laughter.)

Gacheru: 'But, Kasii! he beat the bush like an elephant.'

Ruku: 'It is as though you have never seen Kimathi run before. A .22 wouldn't catch him, probably only a .303! [Laughter.] Even now he is still running and I know his men will look for him for four days.'

Everyone: '*Noguo, noguo.* Even five days.' (Laughter.)

Gacheru: 'But it is very bad for someone to suddenly shout, "Name yourself." And you couldn't possibly see him. You might become too alarmed.'

Gati: 'Aaaaaaah! You must be stupid. Do you think he is not alarmed too when he says that? He is pulling his tail very hard between his legs.'

Rukwaro: 'That is it, for the little mouse squeals when its tail is stood on.' (Laughter.)

Then everyone would talk at the same time and nobody would listen and there would be several minutes of pandemonium. But after a while only the most talkative would keep on.

Gacheru: 'If you hear Kimathi's voice you will be most surprised.'

Njeru: 'Don't you know he was already running when he shouted?'

Thia: 'No, he would be crouched down looking ahead.'

Gacheru: 'There is nothing like that. Even Karau told me that when he shouted his feet were already doing . . .' (Gacheru demonstrated a dog-paddle.) (Laughter.)

Gati: 'None of them will eat for three days now and anyone who touches food with his finger will be killed.'

Everyone: '*Noguo,* that is it absolutely.'

Kibata: 'He will pray and pray and pray.'

Gacheru (standing up): 'What you are doing is not good. You must let me talk. I was there.'

Thia: 'Kimathi might kill two people because of this.'

Everyone: '*Noguo, noguo.*' (Laughter.)

Gacheru: 'Please realize that I was there and for that reason there is only room for me to speak.'

Ruku: '*Noguo*, go ahead, but tie up your words for we have heard them for long enough.'

Wanjau: 'But that woman, she is like lightning.'

Gacheru (annoyed): 'All right, you stand, Wanjau.'

Ruku: 'I don't want to hear anyone talk about Wanjiru. It is too much.'

Kibata: 'That one will never be caught by the bum [their saying for surrender] because she will kill herself first.'

—and so the conversation continued. When they were too tired to sit up, they lay down on the ground and continued talking. When the fires had died down and the cold early morning breeze began to blow, they covered their bodies, and their heads, with empty jute bags, mumbling on to one another until the dawn came.

So operation 'Wild Fig', as we called it, had not been entirely unproductive. Only thirteen members of the gang were left at large. The trap itself had not caught anyone, but the art of trapping had.

Chapter Seventeen

HIS DREAM AT KANJEMA

Iri kanwa itiri nda

Food in the mouth is
not yet in the stomach

or

Do not cry herrings till
they are in the net.

BECAUSE of our growing operational strength, we had to increase our staff. Finding men who had the temperament and liking for this type of work was difficult but there were many volunteers and eight were finally chosen. From the Kenya Regiment came three young soldiers, Bill Eastbrook, Laurie Pearse and Jim Stephen, all Kenya-born, all under twenty, all strong and single. From the Kenya Police came three fit and seasoned men, Colin Leath, Patrick Smith and Dick Crow and two outstanding Africans, Busani, a Mkamba, and Kiprotich, a Nandi.

In a remarkably short space of time all these men had become experts in the delicate task of handling Mau Mau pseudo-terrorists. Busani and Kiprotich had worked with me before, during the emergency, and Leath already had considerable experience in pseudo-gang operations.

Time and time again these young men went into the forest on their own to operate with the teams. Their readiness to face danger when alone with the terrorists and far cut off from their colleagues was admirable. With the aid of these men it was possible to expand the force still further and bring even greater pressure to bear on Kimathi and other terrorists remaining in the forest.

Some days after his capture, Karau told us about a meeting Kimathi had arranged with the gang-leader called Chege Karobia, the terrorist from whom Gati and Hungu had sought shelter when they had fled from Kimathi on the Moorlands. According to Karau, Kimathi had found Chege's game traps towards the end of July and, to fill the gaps in his own ranks, he decided to take over Chege and his followers. The traps were to be the first channel of communication between the two groups. With this take-over in mind he had sent some of his men to sit by the snares and wait for Chege. On the 3rd of August, when two of Chege's men turned up, Kimathi gave them food and sent them away with a letter inviting their leader to a meeting.

A week later, Chege replied and sent word back by the same two men saying that he was ready to meet Kimathi and suggesting a rendezvous on the 26th of August. This news had been kept very secret by Kimathi. Though he told his men about his plan and also about the date, he had been very careful not to tell them where they would meet. As a result, Karau had not the faintest idea where to lead us.

There were now less than one hundred terrorists at large on the Aberdares, but we did not want Kimathi to recruit them.

Luck was now on our side. Two days after Karau gave us his information, Chege Karobia, the only terrorist in the forest who could tell us where the meeting was going to be held, was captured with four other members of his gang by one of our teams operating under Colin Leath. Nothing could have been more timely. We celebrated in the best of traditions!

Chege, who stood barely five foot on his tiptoes, was a terrorist of no little importance. He had been in the jungle since early 1953 and had risen to a level of prominence which entitled him to visit various gangs operating in the western Aberdares and issue instructions to them. He had once been closely associated with Kimathi who (at meetings of the Ituma Demi Trinity Council) had shown an unusual liking for him.

Unlike other Mau Mau who sought refuge in the depths of the forest, he had thought it far safer to hide as near to the forest edge as possible. He had camped close to a large timber mill called Geta at the foot of Kipipiri. He believed that nobody would look for him near a major logging centre where hundreds of civilian Africans were employed. He made no hide-out because the workers from the mill would be certain to find it when they wandered through the woods trying to trap buck. Instead, he slept with his gang near the labour camp and fed on buck taken from the labourers' traps. He never tried to conceal his tracks which were merged with those of the workers and he cooked at night on well-hidden fires which were camouflaged by smoke from the camp kitchens.

The gangs which Chege once controlled had suffered very severely in the last nine months and Kimathi's invitation reached Chege at a time when he was desperately worried about the thought of losing more men. He thought that, at any moment, he might be left alone without anyone to hunt and forage for him and he had, in fact, been greatly comforted by Kimathi's overtures.

As soon as he fell into our hands, we tried to get him to tell us where the rendezvous would be and, knowing that he would not be very pleased to hear of Kimathi's plot, we confronted him with Karau, who made no bones about the fact that there was to be no question of reaching any agreement with Kimathi and that he and his men were to be captured and forced to serve a new master. Chege was furious and he soon began to tell us all about the arrangements he had made for the meeting, which was to take place on a hill called Rurimeria in the central part of the Moorlands. He also told us how both gangs had arranged to use either of two secret letter boxes high on the Aberdares in case something went wrong and the meeting had to be cancelled.

It was clear that the cunning Kimathi had not agreed to anything which would expose him too much. He himself would not be going to Rurimeria. He would send some of his henchmen to meet Chege and they were going to guide Chege to a place where he would be waiting. No one, not even Chege, had the remotest idea where that would be. We were back with our old problem, how to get at Kimathi. Our men couldn't go to the rendezvous on the hill, for they would not be taken on to the next rendezvous. If Chege and his four followers went, they would be powerless, for they had no firearms and we did not trust them enough to arm them ourselves.

With no answer in mind, we set off to carry out a reconnaissance of Rurimeria hill and the surrounding country. We squeezed no less than fourteen team leaders, plus Chege and one of his men, into our Land Rover and we climbed up the Aberdares by the old Fort Jerusalem track and finally stopped by a river called the Karimu where we could see the whole area. After studying the country with my binoculars, which fascinated our terrorists, it was clear that our greatest difficulty was going to be getting into the area unseen. The whole region was dotted with little hillocks and from the top of each one you could watch many miles of the open Moorlands with ease. This meant that we had to move by night. There was no other way.

While we were up there discussing the matter, Gati suggested that we should get Chege to write a letter to Kimathi confirming the fact that he would be attending the meeting come hell or high water. We had failed to make up our minds on anything else, so we happily spent the rest of the day dictating a letter to Kimathi which Chege wrote.

When we reached the first letter box, an isolated mukeu tree, we found that it had been uprooted and smashed by an elephant some time during the previous week. The question of whether the animal had done this because of its dislike for Kimathi, or because of its dislike for Chege, was heatedly argued by our terrorists, but they were at least agreed that we should go on to the second box. This one was also in a tree. After Chege had placed his letter in a hollow, he broke off a branch from a nearby mukoromobothi tree and stuck it in the ground at the base of the letter box. He then went some yards away, broke off another small branch and stuck this one at the foot of a different tree. He told us that he had arranged with Kimathi's messengers that the letter box would not be checked, even if it obviously contained a letter, unless both these branches were in position. The Security Forces could easily plant a fictitious letter, but they would not know about the two branches. That was a secret shared by Chege and Kimathi alone.

As we had all milled around the letter box, Chege very sensibly drew our attention to our tracks. 'What do you suppose Kimathi's men will say when they see the tracks of seventeen people here and they know there are only a total of five of us in my gang?' he asked. 'They will not say anything,' replied Gati, 'they will simply go up into the air like a jet.' When we stopped laughing, we set about the task of removing every superfluous mark within two hundred yards of the tree and this took some time.

It was almost six o'clock when we arrived back at our Land Rover on the Karimu river.

That evening as we were leaving the Moorlands, we encountered some old friends—six waterbuck. These old faithfuls had been in that very locality for the past eighteen months and I had never once been through the area without seeing them. They had become almost part of the landscape and I often thought how unfortunate it was that they could not tell us about Kimathi and the hundreds of other terrorists who must have passed before their eyes.

When we arrived back at our base camp, I suddenly realized that Kimathi might tell his confederates where the meeting was going to be held, and realizing that nothing could then cancel his plans more certainly than the capture of one of his men, I decided to withdraw all our teams from the forest as quickly as possible. For the first time since our operations began, we did not want to lay hands on any of Kimathi's followers.

In the next few days at our Mayfield camp, we racked our brains to find a foolproof plan for dealing with the meeting, but whichever way we looked at the problem, we found that there was no alternative to sending Chege and his four men to make the initial contact on the hill. As Kimathi knew that they had no guns, they would have to go unarmed. But what were we going to do once Chege had made his contact? Somehow we had to find a way of trailing the party on the hill until they reached Kimathi.

The decision to send Chege and his companions alone did not please them. They were petrified at the thought of going unarmed to meet Kimathi's men. 'If you want to finish us,' said Chege, 'finish us here, but do not send us to be finished by Kimathi.' After a great deal of persuasion they finally agreed to go, provided the area was completely surrounded by our men and that this force was so deployed that the meeting point on the hill would be kept under continuous observation from all sides.

With all this in mind we drew up our final plans. At ten o'clock on the morning of the meeting, Chege and his men would travel over the open ground so that, from a distance, they could be counted and identified by Kimathi's men. The night before, sixteen well-armed teams would have moved up through the forest onto the Moorlands and, covered by the darkness, they would surround the hill about a mile from its summit. Each team would be five strong so that, if their tracks were seen, Kimathi's men would assume they were Chege's. The positions that the teams would take up would enable at least half of them to watch the meeting place on Rurimeria throughout the hours of daylight, and at least three teams would be able to trail the party which-ever side of the hill they ultimately went down. After the two gangs had met—when Chege was being led away to Kimathi—our men would follow them at a discreet dis-tance. If Kimathi was hiding so far away that the party had not arrived before dusk, Kimathi's guides were to be captured and made to reveal where their leader was lying up. We could do no more.

During the night of the 25th of August, our force was dropped off in pitch darkness at the bottom of the Marishimiti gorge on the west side of the Aberdares. There was a last-minute shuffling about as they checked their arms and crowded round their leaders, then each leader had a final word to say to Chege, who, in turn, had much to say to them—his life depended on their alert-ness. Before they set off up the mountain for Rurimeria, which was eleven miles away, every man came up and shook hands with us. There were hands which were hard and rough like the bark of a log; there were others which were sticky with filth and honey; some hands were deformed while others were firm and confident.

Here in the dark forest three Europeans were shaking hands with nearly a hundred well-armed Mau Mau who, only a short while before, would have much enjoyed murdering us. While I personally never thought that any of them wanted to do us harm, for we had turned them psychologically until they would willingly have given their lives for us, I was deeply conscious of one possible weak link—a supernatural omen which they might interpret as a sign of Ngai's wrath. It could be an earth tremor, it could be a particularly bright meteorite falling through the atmosphere, it could be an unusual sound in the forest, it could be snakes falling from a tree, or it could be anything else which was weird and uncommon. Little things could have a disastrous effect upon such highly superstitious people. The risk was small, very, very small, but it was present and its presence was enough to cause anxiety. Only a year or so before thousands of them had been ready to accept our bid to get them to surrender. Then a terrorist had found one small red prayer-book written in some Oriental language which they could not understand. Perhaps it had fallen from a plane. Perhaps a soldier had dropped it. Perhaps it had slipped out of someone's pack. But a group of witch-doctors decided that the book had been dropped by Ngai to tell them to remain in the forest and the surrender talks broke down. We were always vulnerable to evil spirits.

Soon the teams left us and a feeling of uncertain expectancy descended upon those of us who were waiting. There were many things to worry about but nothing positive could now be done about any of them. In this state of mind we could not sleep, nor could we stop talking about our fears and our hopes. The night passed slowly and eventually none of us had anything more to say. One by one we moved away to sit or lie down and think in silence until dawn came, with the warming sun and the greater confidence that heat brings.

By dawn all the teams were in position round Ruri-meria hill and at ten o'clock Chege and his gang began their final approach. Across the Moorlands they came in single file; as they climbed the hillside every one of them could be seen by our men but when they reached the top there was no sign of any of Kimathi's henchmen. They could do nothing but sit down and wait.

All day they waited patiently, walking about the top every hour or so to show the teams around them that they were still there, but nobody turned up. That night, when they realized they could be captured and taken away without our teams knowing anything about it, they moved halfway down the hill and lay silently, ready to run at the first sign of someone approaching. But by dawn there was still no sign of Kimathi's men. They thought he had probably made a mistake in his dates, and would be coming during the next day, but as before, this was not to be. Throughout the third day and night they were still lying there, and the teams were still in formation around them, and still nobody came.

By this time those of us lower down the mountain and out of contact with the situation were becoming very worried. First we imagined that they must have contacted Kimathi and were pursuing him, but we could not understand why, if this was so, our men had not sent a runner to tell us what was happening, as they usually did. Then we imagined that our teams must still be waiting round the hill, but this also seemed unlikely as our men knew how punctual the Mau Mau were and it would be most unusual for them to wait even one day longer than the specified date.

On the afternoon of the fourth day, tired, weary and very hungry after their long, unproductive ambush, all our teams left their positions and set off down the mountain towards us, withdrawing Chege and his gang *en route*. Some hours later they reached us, exhausted. 'This is another thing to me,' said Gati on arrival. 'The Mau Mau never fail to keep an arrangement unless an operation is going on.' I suggested that the tracks of our men or the teams themselves had probably been seen. 'There is nothing like that and even Kimathi will confirm what I say when we catch him,' replied Gati.

When we arrived back at Mayfield camp the following day, our team leaders, ever suspicious of anything said or done by Kimathi's gangsters who had misled them so many times before, immediately pounced on Karau and accused him of having known all the time where the meeting was to have taken place. They were certain that Kimathi would have turned up if someone from his gang, who knew his secret, had not been captured. As Karau was the last member of the gang to fall into our hands, they presumed that he must have known far more than he told us. 'When another man is caught ask him and if he says I knew about that, you may kill me,' he said. '*Noguo, noguo*,' agreed the team leaders. 'That is exactly what we will do.'

However, it was not long before we had our next contact with the gang and captured more prisoners from whom we were able to discover the reason for Kimathi's failure to attend the meeting. It turned out that he had been determined to go to Rurimeria hill right up until the very last moment. He had crossed the Honi river, then the Chania river and had slept the night of the 25th of August in the Kanjema area on the Moorlands where there are many small lakes. As Kanjema was only some four miles from Rurimeria, he had no distance to travel the following day. What is more, he had even planned to go himself to meet Chege on the hilltop just in case any of his men were frightened of 'snatching' the party because it contained another leader. But during the night, while he and all his men and Wanjiru were asleep on a small island in the centre of one of the lakes, he had suddenly awoken in a state of great alarm and ordered everyone to get up and move on. His men pleaded with him to wait until the dawn before he moved but he was adamant. He told them he had had a dream in which he had seen himself captured on a hill and that had decided him. In the freezing cold of the night, he and his gang waded through the water and trekked across the Moorlands. By dawn they had reached the forest on the eastern side of the mountain. Once again, his dreams had saved his life.

The spirits that warned Kimathi of impending danger were certainly not able to soothe his temper once his nerves were jangling. His behaviour in the days following his dream at Kanjema amounted to a reign of terror.

As he headed back from Kanjema he walked some fifty yards behind his men. Not even Wanjiru, his favourite, was allowed near him. He strode along with his hands on his hips as he always did when he was annoyed, and from his erratic shambling walk it was obvious to his men that he was crazed with temper. Twice they slowed to make sure that he was still behind and twice, as he came up to them, he raged at them, abused them, threatened them, and chased them on. Just before dawn, his men came to an abrupt stop as he screamed at them, '*Hiti ici, mwathie ku?*' ('You hyenas, where are you going?') Without waiting for him to come up, they altered course and went on. Kimathi did not often shout at night.

As Chege was approaching the top of Rurimeria hill, Kimathi arrived at the place which was to be his lair for

the next two days. The site was less than three miles
from one of his prayer trees, the Kinaini river was a mile
to the south and behind the hide-out was a deep crater
nearly seventy yards long and thirty yards wide. From a
defensive point of view, he could not have chosen a
better place. He could only be approached by climbing the steep side of the crater, which was jagged and
slippery.

As soon as he arrived, he snatched a rifle from the
shoulder of one of his men and ordered two of his followers, Gitahi and Maragua, to accompany him into the
forest. There they sat down. For some minutes he was
silent and looked only at the ground in front of him, but
then he slowly raised his head and stared at the two terrorists. Throughout the forest it was known that when
Kimathi stared at a man the victim would freeze with
terror. Death glimmered in his wide, bloodshot eyes,
reddened by the bhang, or wild tobacco, which he habi-
tually put in them. Many times before, a glare from these
eyes had made a terrorist beg for mercy before a word
had been spoken. Gitahi and Maragua were sure that
they would die. Trembling with anger, Kimathi held
out his right hand and pointed to one of his fingers. 'How
many joints are there in this finger?' 'Three,' replied
Gitahi. 'Asorite,' answered Kimathi, using the pidgin
English he often spoke when trying to impress his
listeners. He then went on to tell them that he was the
first joint, nearest the blood and therefore nearest to
Ngai; Gitahi was the second because he was trustworthy,
he had been captured by the enemy and then escaped;
Maragua was the third joint, affixed to the others 'like
an unborn child to its mother'. Because of that, Kimathi
continued, they were his 'eyes and strength' and they
were to stand by him until they all died together. Gitahi
and Maragua were pleased to hear this. Even Ngai, they

thought, could not have bestowed a greater honour upon them.

Still shaking with anger, Kimathi ordered his two favourites to fetch another terrorist named Githua and soon this unfortunate man was brought along, his wrists bound with trapping wires. When Githua stood before him, Kimathi rose to his feet, spat on the ground to clear his throat and began accusing Githua of treachery. He gave Githua no chance to answer. For several minutes the outburst continued. Where had Githua been when he went off to contact Chege Karobia some weeks before, he had been away a very long time. Was it not clear that he had taken the opportunity of betraying them all to the enemy? Githua pleaded with Kimathi to let him speak but it was no good. 'I even saw you in my dream telling the white men about the meeting at Rurimeria,' Kimathi claimed. The 'trial' was over. Githua was tackled and thrown to the ground where he was pinned down. A trapping wire was then forced over his head and Kimathi tightened the noose with both his hands. Githua's eyes widened, he spluttered, his limbs shook and stretched, his tonguecurled outof his mouth.Then his body was dragged away and stuffed down an antbear hole. Kimathi enjoyed pushing his victims into antbear holes.

After this, Kimathi returned to the hide-out where the rest of his followers were sitting silently. They knew from the expression on his face that Githua was dead but they felt neither sympathy for their ex-colleague nor anger with Kimathi. Their own lives, they thought, had been saved by Kimathi's dream and if he had seen that Githua was a traitor he must have been one. Kimathi's dreams were infallible. Nevertheless they were worried. They were tormented by the thought that they might have done something unknowingly which was also wrong in

Kimathi's eyes, which he would see in his dreams, and which would send them along the road taken by all his victims—into the antbear hole, head first, and dead.

Kimathi's eyes were quick to find fault. He was looking for trouble. While Githua's trial had been in progress, Wanjiru had remained with the men instead of sitting apart where they could not 'disease her mind'. He believed he was the only male who could talk to a woman without ruining her. When he discovered that she had stayed with the men, he gripped her by the wrist and dragged her off to the edge of the crater. There he thrashed her with a bamboo stick and demanded that she should tell him what the men had said to her. In his own words, she had to 'tahikia ndeto thuku' or vomit out the words which were spoiling her mind.

Leaving Wanjiru crying on the ground, he came back into the hide-out where he made yet another awesome row, this time with his favourite Gitahi, who had stupidly cut three munyamate sticks to support the cooking pot over the fire. They all knew that this type of wood would quickly catch fire in the flames and let the cooking pot fall into the fire.

Nothing pleased Kimathi. He threatened his men several times. He told them that when they next made a mistake he would re-oath them by making them eat Githua's intestines which they would have to dig out of the antbear hole. He nicked his finger with a knife and while it was bleeding placed it in a gourd of water so that his blood could be drunk by all present. 'When you drink my blood,' he said, 'your foolishness will disappear and you will have sense like me.'

When the sun had set and darkness fell, Kimathi went away and lay down beneath the trunk of a fallen tree. He had a rifle on one side and a revolver on the other. Throughout the night he tossed and turned in the grip of a nightmare. At times he sat up abruptly and looked around for a minute or two before lying down to sleep again. His men sat watching him. Once when he groaned very loudly some suggested going over to find out if he was in trouble, but they knew he had gone to lie beneath the tree so that nobody could strike at him and they knew he had taken the guns because he feared that he would be attacked. If they went near him, therefore, he would be sure to think that they were coming to kill him and they would be shot for their trouble. He was best left alone to toss and turn until a new day had dawned.

One of the most remarkable things about Kimathi's gang was the implicit loyalty of his followers. They never plotted against him despite his savagery to them. He might lick his lips at the thought of killing them, but they never dreamt of shooting him as he slept. Kimathi, however, did not seem to realize how safe he was, for whenever he murdered one of his men, or swore at them or beat them, he took great care to see that his own men did not get a chance to attack him without warning. If he had known how difficult we found it to get his men to co-operate with us, he would, perhaps, have been less suspicious of them.

At the first glimmer of dawn, Kimathi rose and set off alone to study the behaviour of the partridges. He believed, as did most other Mau Mau, that if partridges took to wing and scattered as soon as human beings came upon them, the day would end in tragedy. On the other hand, if they scurried along the ground for a few yards before flying away, they would be showing the muirigo or the way and this was an omen of good fortune. When he returned to the hide-out, he was in a better frame of mind and his followers knew that the partridges must have scurried.

As there was only a little decomposed buck meat left

from the food the gang had carried to Kanjema and back,
he told some of his men to go off to look for honey while
others were detailed to go and search for buck paths in
the forest. By evening everyone was back again, but their
reports were not good. There was no honey in the area
and there were too many wild pig about who would
break the trapping wires as soon as they were snared.
Once again Kimathi grew angry and jeered at his men
for being no better than women. As darkness fell he took
Ngunyi aside to listen to the animal noises in the forest
and asked him what the animals were saying, but whenever Ngunyi confessed ignorance or gave an opinion
which differed from Kimathi's, he too was called a
woman.

Some time that night—nobody had any idea what time
it was—Kimathi ordered his gang to break camp and
move on. They crossed the Kinaini river, and then the
Muringato river, on their way to a cave once used by
Juma Abdalla as a food store. But when they reached it
they found it was empty. All the food had been cleared
out by our teams some time before. So on Kimathi and
his followers went until they reached that part of the
jungle which they called Mathakwa-ini.

During the next few days when new game traps were
being laid, the gang grew more and more hungry. The
few fruit-yielding trees were bare. Most of the bees had
eaten their honey during the misty period and had not
replenished their hives. Meat was, as yet, unobtainable
as their traps were only now going up. What little food
they did find was given to Kimathi and Wanjiru. Three
hyrax were caught in an ingenious but cruel way. When
their holes in the trees were discovered, a long, pliant
stick, spliced at the tip, was thrust up the hole until the
hyrax felt the tip boring into their bodies and screeched.
Then the terrorists turned the stick so that the soft woolly

hair of the animals was wound round the tip. They were
then pulled down, clubbed to death and given to Kimathi and Wanjiru. For the other members of the gang, lack
of food soon became a desperate problem. Old buckskin
garments were boiled and eaten after the hair had been
scraped off, rats were welcome morsels, while some roots
were dug up and boiled for their juices. The gangsters took
it in turn to sit near their game traps to make sure that,
when a buck was caught, it would not be eaten by hyenas
or leopards. Spurred on by hunger, Kimathi's men were
sitting in pairs by their widely-scattered traps. They were
still sitting there when our operations began again after
the abortive operation of Rurimeria hill and in the first
week of September we caught four more of Kimathi's
men. All four were sitting beside game traps when the
teams found them and none had eaten any food for
several days. We did everything possible to get them to
tell us where Kimathi was lurking, but, like the other cap-
tives, they were sullen and silent until they were sure
that their disappearance had been noticed and that
Kimathi had been given ample time to move himself, his
gang and his traps to a different place. Then they started
talking and we heard all about his dream at Kanjema,
about his reign of terror and about Githua's death.

Even before Githua's death the gang had been cut to
thirteen and you might have thought that this alone
would prevent Kimathi from killing any more of his
men. But what was logic to others was not logic to him.
Githua's death had reduced his strength to twelve and
the capture of the four men at the traps brought him
down to the meagre total of eight. As Gati said, Kimathi's
organization was 'rotting from the head and from the tail
at the same time'.

The revelations of the last terrorists to fall into our
hands crowned our unceasing efforts to convince our men

who came from Kimathi's home district of Nyeri that he was a maniac who would, in time, kill all those who followed him. Our men from Nyeri and our men from Fort Hall were now equally keen to hunt the chief leader of Mau Mau to his end.

Chapter Eighteen

THE DOWNWARD SLOPE

Wa moru unungaga uri thiaka

A wicked man's arrow emits its
unpleasant smell even if hidden
in the quiver.

THE 15th of September dawned without a cloud in the
sky. It was one of those days which leave a lasting impression of Kenya's beauty on your mind. As the sun came up
behind the snow-capped peak of Mount Kenya, we were
climbing the Aberdares from the west, facing into the
sun. Eleven Land Rovers, carrying twelve teams, were
winding their way slowly over the Moorlands towards
the eastern slopes. This time we were entering the
Kimathi area by the back door to give ourselves the
benefit of working downhill.

The beauty of our hunting ground was overpowering.
We were on top of the world, above the sun, looking
down on a vast land of valleys, forests and hills which
were blanketed by a warm purple shadow. The night
had been starry and clear so that there was frost on the
hillsides which glittered against a background of greens,
violets and blues. All the little streams stood out like
pencil lines on a map, the waterfalls sparkled white in
the sunshine and a gentle breeze waved the heather softly
from side to side. Even the moorland trees looked spry
as their long grey creepers (old men's beards, we called
them) swung peacefully backwards and forwards.

As we drove along we found rhino and buffalo warming themselves in the open glades. Where they were very close to the track, the vehicles fanned out to allow for sudden acceleration if any of the animals should charge, and the terrorists kept peering under the canvas canopies at the backs of the vehicles ready to raise the alarm.

One of our main sources of amusement, apart from swapping stories about our escapes from rhino, was the little brown Jackson's francolin. In this high country these birds have small feathers growing under the scales of their legs, giving them an odd, morris-dancing look. Gati was convinced that 'God had given them socks' to protect their legs from the cold and as we journeyed along, he gave a running commentary on the value and quality of the socks each one was wearing.

Every so often we came to particularly tricky parts of the track, where the vehicles tilted precariously on an extremely slippery surface. Sometimes there was a real danger that the vehicles would tumble down considerable precipices. As a rule, we stopped the Land Rovers before trying to cross these patches and we would let the passengers get out of the backs so that if the skill of the driver failed he could plummet down the steep slope alone. But as they were not sure that the vehicles would stop to allow them to get out, the terrorists struggled frantically whenever a bad spot came in sight. It was a lively ride.

Further across the Moorlands and nearer the forest were three elephant skulls, all lying within a few feet of one another. The animals may have been killed by the bombing or even by Kimathi with his elephant gun in the earlier days of the emergency. But whatever the cause of their deaths, they served as a vital landmark, for if a Land Rover went more than a few hundred yards past

H

them, it could be seen by anyone in the Kimathi area far down below. This was our off-loading point.

Before we finally stopped that day, I vowed, as I had vowed many times before, that when I was an old man I would return to the Aberdares and sit up there on the Moorlands and dream of the days gone by—of our operations, of the beauty and magnificence of this part of the world which is, as yet, untouched by civilization. And I hoped that when that time came, the skeletons of the dead and the scars of war would have disappeared and only the beauty of this wonderful land would remain.

When the teams had got out and the vehicles had been tucked away behind the thickest bushes, we set off, on foot, down the eastern slope of the mountain. When we reached the thick bamboo, all but one of the teams branched off to their destinations; the last we held back in reserve. They went in four separate groups. One was to wind its way down to the Kinaini river and ambush two mugumo trees where we thought Kimathi might soon be going to pray; another, guided by one of the most recently captured members of the gang, was to visit the hide-out where Kimathi had last been seen in case he had left any tracks; the third was to search the Mathak-wa-ini area of forest for game traps, for this was where he was most likely to be hunting; and the last was to travel right down the mountain, a journey of nearly twenty-six miles, until they reached the edge of the forest bordering the Nyeri native reserve where they were to search for the tracks of foraging parties. Because of the grave shortage of food in the gang, we felt that Kimathi might have taken the unusual course of sending some of his men into the Kikuyu reserve to steal food and we might pick up their tracks along the fringe of the forest.

During the first two days of the operation we made no contacts—and one of our terrorists was badly injured by a rhino. At the mugumo tree near the Kinaini river, there were some fairly recent tracks which showed that Kimathi was still praying, but there was no honey beneath the trees. For once his belly had come before his god, and he had eaten the honey rather than spill it as an offering to Ngai. The hide-out was empty, apart from a few scattered pieces of boiled buckskin which had obviously proved too tough to eat, and there were no clear tracks worth following. In the Mathakwa-ini area, the third group found several places where buck traps had been laid, and then lifted. It was clear that he had been trapping there but he had moved on when he found that more of his men had been captured. The fourth group found the tracks of two men and followed them in high hopes, but when these circled back to the reserve after passing some old, empty honey hives, it was clear that they belonged to Kikuyu living in the reserve and not to Mau Mau. These Kikuyu had probably wanted the honey for marital negotiations, possibly to appease some irate father who was being offered too small a dowry for his daughter. If that were so, their need was indeed great, but they were treading on dangerous ground.

On the 17th of September our luck changed. Beside a small, muddy pool near Ruhuru-ini our men spotted the toe marks of a single terrorist, who had drawn water the day before, and all approaches to the pool were ambushed in the hope that he would return. As the ambushers lay there, troop after troop of baboons came down to water. Then, round about two o'clock in the afternoon, a lone terrorist was seen approaching the pool, where several baboons were still drinking. The animals saw him and snarled and barked, but refused to give way. For several minutes the terrorist, who might easily have passed for a baboon himself with his long hair and dirty brown skin coat, threw stones and sticks at the animals to try to frighten them away, but each time he attacked, two or three of the larger baboons rushed at him and chased him back into the forest. This, it seemed, was a feud between equals, where each party was claiming his right and was fighting for it; where, unless one gave way, there would be a fight to the finish. After the ambushers had watched the conflict for some time, they crept up behind the terrorist. He was concentrating so hard on his argument with the baboons that he did not notice them until the very last moment. For some time the baboons did not see our men either, then the terrorist suddenly sensed danger and, on looking round, saw our men crawling up, but it was too late for our target.

That same day the tracks of three men were picked up by another of our groups not far from Wuthering Heights, at least thirty miles to the north-west, and thanks to Gacheru and his outstanding tracking ability, these were followed to a letter box in the Mwathe sector. As our men arrived, they caught a glimpse of the three terrorists leaving it. Unfortunately our men were also seen and in a split second the Mau Mau had darted away. Fanning out into a long line, the teams sped after them. After running three or four hundred yards, they saw the terrorists on the opposite side of a valley climbing up the steep slope. Some of our men raced on after them, but others stood on the high ground and shouted across the valley to some imaginary colleagues: 'Stay where you are. They are going straight for you.' This bluff worked. Two of the terrorists must have been so busy running that they did not hear the shouting, but the third stopped suddenly, looked up at the top of the hill for a few seconds, then turned right and charged down into the valley again. Here he collided with our men who dived at him. For a few moments he fought like a cat. He had been grabbed by five or six of our men, most of whom were

cut with his simi or were severely bitten on their hands
and he only gave up after someone hit him hard on the
head with a Patchett magazine. Mbaka is the Kikuyu
word for cat and this, appropriately, was his name.

It turned out that he and three others, one of whom
was the unfortunate wretch being chivvied by the baboons, had been sent off by Kimathi three days before
to look for new trapping wires which the gang needed
badly. They had gone to examine the wreckage of an
aircraft east of the National Park track where they hoped
they would be able to remove some of the electrical
wiring. They got to the scene of the crash without mishap, but when they examined the crumbling mass of
metal from a safe distance, they thought they saw a
booby-trap and left the scene hurriedly.

They had not gone far, however, before they were
charged by a rhino with calf in that same terrible part of
the Tree Tops salient which we had all come to dread,
and all four terrorists ran in different directions. It was
quite some time before the angry rhino moved on and
Mbaka could emerge from his hiding place to rally his
men, but he could only find two of them. For two hours
Mbaka searched for the missing terrorist unsuccessfully,
before deciding that he must have gone back to rejoin
Kimathi at the hide-out, so they headed for the hide-out
themselves.

To their intense surprise, they arrived to find the hide-
out deserted. Not only was the missing terrorist not there,
but Kimathi and the rest of the gang were not there
either. Furthermore, the place had obviously been abandoned for good. That night Mbaka and his two companions lay in the hide-out wondering how they could
find Kimathi again and early the next morning they
began to look for him. Day and night they searched.
Without food and without trapping wires, they began to

think they might die of hunger unless they could make contact with Kimathi again, but they found no trace of him. They were still searching when our men saw them at the letter box. They had been all the way to Wuthering Heights and back, a journey of nearly seventy miles over rough country.

The story told by the lone terrorist captured at the pool confirmed all that Mbaka told us. Like the others, he had run when the rhino charged and then returned to look for his companions when the animal had moved away. Somehow, they missed each other. That night he slept in a tree and the following day set off for the hide-out alone. Everyone had gone. By this time even Mbaka had come and gone.

Lonely and hungry, he decided to go on looking for Mbaka but not for Kimathi, definitely not Kimathi. He had been alone. There was no one to corroborate his story and the unbelieving Kimathi would think he had betrayed the others to the enemy and was now coming back in the hope of betraying everyone else. For that he knew he would be strangled and pushed down an antbear hole. Even if Mbaka had got back to Kimathi and supported his story about the rhino, who could say that, since that time, he had not turned traitor and passed information to the Security Forces? The odds were against him and he knew he had to avoid Kimathi at all costs. So he drank where the baboons drank, in a filthy, muddy, stagnant pool fouled by baboon excreta and urine, for that was one place his leader was unlikely to go to.

With two more of his gang accounted for, Kimathi was now left with only six followers. There was his treasured woman, Wanjiru; there were his two favourites, the two joints of his finger, Gitahi and Maragua; and there were three others for whom he had no special affection, Ngunyi, Kondia and 7 Kar.

Mbaka told us that in his last week with Kimathi, he had twice heard his leader speak of suicide, of going away to some remote part of the mountain with Wanjiru where he would first shoot her and then shoot himself. He had told his men that his body would not be found by his enemies as it would be a sin 'against the bones of his grandmother' if he were taken out of the forest. When he had last talked of death, he had called for his goat-skin satchel and from it he had removed all his documents. There were twenty or thirty old letters from other terrorist leaders as well as his small diary, the diary in which the names of all those to be executed were recorded. Sitting before a fire, he had read the letters to those around him. Only Wanjiru, being a woman, had to sit aside, for she was forbidden to hear such things. As he read each letter, he threw it into the flames and watched it roll up, blacken and then catch fire. When all this had been done, he picked up his copy of *Napoleon's Book of Charms*. This had been torn by a bullet during the battle with Gacheru's team when they captured Karau and his partner near the bomb crater. Putting the charm book on his lap, he flicked the pages over, then, with his last stub pencil, he worked out what the future held for him. His men looked on in silence, anxious to hear the result, for his fate was their fate, but when he had finished, he told them nothing. He ripped the pages from the book one by one and threw them onto the fire like the letters. Now they knew they were near the bottom of the downward slope.

Mbaka also told us about a last sacrifice Kimathi intended to stage near the top of Mount Kinangop, about eighty miles to the south. As he could not get a live goat for the ceremony, he had decided to use a live buck, one of those caught in his traps. He proposed to place earth in the eyes of the animal and then sew up its eye-

lids with forest thorns and twine to show that the land
was dear to him; then he intended to slit the animal's
ear so that its blood would pour over the rocks as an
offering to Ngai; finally, before the animal was dead, he
planned to bury it with its head pointing upwards to
signify 'the rising of his fortune'.

When all arrangements had been completed for the
ceremony, he called his men round him and questioned
them about the safest route to Mount Kinangop, but
none could advise him. They all knew, however, that it
would be dangerous to move before the partridges gave
them the 'all clear'. That same evening, therefore,
Kimathi and the remnants of his gang went through the
forest to see how the birds would behave. They came
upon two flocks, but in each case, instead of scurrying
along the ground, the birds took to the air. After this
bad omen the expedition was cancelled and all-night
prayers were held thanking Ngai for this warning.

Chapter Nineteen

'HOT SCRUM'

Iri kuhuma ndiri muti itangigwaterera

There is no tree to which a panting man
would not cling.

WHEN Gati and Hungu came to us nine months before,
we did not really think that every Mau Mau gang leader
in the Aberdares would fall before Dedan Kimathi.
Thurura, who had long before predicted that Kimathi
would be the last surviving terrorist on the mountain, was
being proved depressingly accurate.

By the middle of September, there were only two Mau
Mau leaders left in the forest, Dedan Kimathi and
Kimani Kimarua. All the others, with the single exception of Stanley Mathenge, who left the mountain long
before, had been eliminated by their former followers
working for us. Kahiu Itina had surrendered quietly
after the fantastic dream of his witch-doctor, Kingori;
Ndungu Gicheru was seized after the brutal ham-string-
ing of the cattle; Kimbo, the singer and cattle thief, had
been swept up with all his gangsters and sentenced to
death for murder; Mururu and Kariuki Kagera, who
had tormented the farmers in the Kinangop, had fallen;
Chege came in and took us on the abortive operation to
Rurimeria; Abdalla, Jeriko, Wambararia and Karau,
from Kimathi's gang, had fallen like skittles to the cunning of their one-time companions; Muraya and Kiiru
had been ambushed in the upper Fort Hall forests;

H*

Njackwema from the far north had been eliminated—and others too had gone the same way. Only Kimathi and Kimani Kimarua remained. But on the 20th of that month of September, Kimani Kimarua was killed in a fight with one of our teams and Kimathi was left as the only considerable terrorist at large in an area where, three years before, nearly twelve thousand Mau Mau and some two hundred major and minor leaders had operated.

Kimani had never been closely associated with Kimathi, nor did his gang ever trespass in the Kimathi area. Some of his men had once brushed with Kimathi's gang on the Moorlands and one had been run to ground and killed. Before that, in June 1955, Kimani had himself been a prisoner of Kimathi with several other Mau Mau leaders including Stanley Mathenge, all of whom Kimathi seized for taking part in surrender talks with Government officers against his wishes. For this offence they had been sentenced to death, bound hand and foot, and placed under guard in a small bamboo hut to await execution at dawn. But during the night a woman terrorist, who was a friend of Stanley Mathenge, entered the hut to take water to the prisoners and cut their bonds. They rushed out, overpowered the guards, seized their weapons and disappeared into the darkness.

After these two clashes, Kimani had no wish to set eyes on Kimathi again, so he went far south into the deep gorge of the Mathioya river. Yet in some ways, these two were not unalike. Kimani had gone into the forest with two brothers; so had Kimathi. Kimani had led his brothers a miserable life in the jungle; so had Kimathi. But unlike Kimathi, Kimani had an unfaithful brother. He was called Ngai, after the Kikuyu god, and he was a member of our force.

Since early childhood Ngai had been beaten and bullied and in the forest he led a very hard life. Kimani used to whip him without reason in front of other members of the gang and he was always ordered to go on the most dangerous expeditions. Ngai had not forgotten this and when he was captured by one of our teams early in September, he was only too anxious to hunt for his brother, who was trapping near the headwaters of the Mathioya river at the time. While operations against Kimathi went on in the north, Ngai searched for his brother in the south.

A few days after Ngai's team, which was led by a most efficient but painfully ugly team leader named Kubwa, had arrived at the upper reaches of the Mathioya river, they came upon a place in the forest where a branch of some large-leafed plant had been cut and left on an animal path. Further down the path they found a similar branch and then another and another. Our men followed on and by nightfall had reached the hide-out where Kimani and two others were resting.

Kimani was sleeping between his two followers, who were tied round the ankles without difficulty, but when the rope touched Kimani's feet, he sprang from the ground, grabbed Kubwa's Patchett by the muzzle and almost wrenched it from his hands. The tug of war did not last long. Kubwa squeezed the trigger and a stream of bullets ripped Kimani's chest at point-blank range.

Ngai was overjoyed when he saw his brother fall. He trotted over to the body and happily ruffled through his dead brother's clothes for any valuables he could find. Mau Mau had taught him, like all others who had succumbed to its doctrine, to have no feelings for kith and kin. He pocketed Kimani's torn and tattered notebook, a little bottle containing antbear fat, which was thought to be a cure for rheumatism, and a small skin wallet which had nothing in it. Then he stripped all the blood-stained garments from his brother's body and slipped them over his own.

The ease with which the team had been able to discover the hide-out made Kubwa ask his two prisoners why they had left the branches along the path. He was told that while a fourth member of the gang had been away setting a game snare, two rifle shots had been heard in the direction of the Gikira river and Kimani had decided to move immediately to a new hide-out. The trail of branches had been left behind so that the trapper would be able to find the new hide-out. As Kubwa told them: 'Had I been born as stupid as you I would have committed suicide long ago!'

That night, the 20th of September, the team remained in the hide-out with their two prisoners and the dead body of Kimani, on the off-chance that the trapper had not heard the firing and would return. That is exactly what he did. He walked unsuspectingly into the ambush just before nine o'clock in the morning.

Now that Dedan Kimathi was the only terrorist of importance on the whole mountain, we decided to ignore the few leaderless oddments scattered here and there and use every man we had in the main hunt.

In the Mwathe and the Tree Tops Salient, Kimathi had three operative letter boxes and by the end of September we knew them all. The first was a hollow beneath the roots of a large tree low down the salient, close to the famous Tree Tops game look-out. The second was about six miles further up the mountain, due west, between the Muringato and Itha rivers in a derelict beehive that had been hanging on a tree for some twenty years. The third was a cavity in a rock some seven miles north-west of this beehive, in the Mwathe area, close to that part of the forest where we had once staged our deception operation.

The last of these would probably not be used again as some of our collaborators knew it well, but the others were almost certain to be used if the gang was split up and wished to communicate with one another.

Kimathi also had two thitoo or food stores, both deep in the forest. One was Juma Abdalla's cave beside the Muringato river, but Kimathi knew that it was now empty. The second, however, was newly dug under a large fig tree in the Ruhotie valley. It had been found and left intact by one of our teams during the last days of the previous operation. We knew that no one would construct a food store in the forest unless there was food to be stored in it. We knew that Kimathi had not obtained food from outside the forest, for we would have found his tracks along the forest edge, so we presumed that his traps were now paying dividends and that he was, at long last, getting so much meat that he was able to dry some for storage. Where, then, were his traps?

The area north of the Ruhotie valley was too close to the farming country of Mweiga; the area to the west of this contained many giant forest hog and was therefore equally unsuitable; the land to the east towards Nyeri and the Polo Ground was a poor trapping area as the forest was sparse and buck wandered about willy-nilly instead of keeping to set paths; but the area to the south of the Ruhotie valley was excellent for trapping at this time of year and it was, we noted, close to his new store. That was where we would look.

Then there were his prayer trees. By discounting all those known to terrorists captured from his gang, we were able to eliminate all but nine. Those who knew him well were positive that these nine were the only ones he would visit again. All the others we could safely forget about.

This analysis gave us *fourteen* key points where we

would look for Kimathi: two letter boxes, two food stores, nine prayer trees and a trapping area. Our hunting ground was narrowed to fifty square miles of forest. Never before had we possessed such full and exact information on which to base an operation and never before had we been blessed with such an expert body of hunters to carry out the task. We were sure that the day of Kimathi's downfall was near. Nobody said very much but everyone was confident.

On the last day of September, our whole force was withdrawn from the forest to prepare for a final, major effort to begin on the 7th of October. This operation was given the expressive code name 'Hot Scrum'. Hour after hour details of the plan were discussed and re-discussed. Day after day we glanced up anxiously at the sky for signs of a change of weather. The rains were due again and it was imperative that we should establish ourselves beside the fourteen key points before they broke. We knew that if we moved through the forest in force after they had started, our tracks would be seen and Kimathi would know that we had found his key points.

On the 3rd of October there was an ominous cluster of dark clouds over Mount Kenya, but by the late evening the sky was clear again. Then on the 4th of October clouds gathered in the north, where some light rain fell, but the Aberdares were spared. Twice we telephoned the Meteorological Department and received a very technical and complicated account of pressure belts and other phenomena, but we had no precise answer to the question we were interested in—when was it going to rain? On the 5th there was a low mist throughout most parts of the Central Province and we breathed a sigh of relief because in East Africa the rains are invariably preceded by extremely hot, sunny days.

In operations of this size and nature, success is

dependent on a great many factors over many of which there is little or no control. The essence, however, consists of keeping the area completely quiet until the operation starts. Activities which would normally have little or no bearing on the conduct of ordinary operations, such as a plane circling over the area, a shot fired on the forest edge, Africans cutting firewood, a fish warden visiting a trout stream, a vehicle bumping up one of the forest tracks or even torches being flashed towards the forest might have a disastrous effect on the outcome of these operations. Every abnormal sound or incident could alter Kimathi's plans and every normal sound or happening could be misconstrued and made to appear abnormal. You could not be too meticulous about the precautions you took to keep the area quiet.

Under these circumstances almost as much work had to go into pre-operational preparations as was put into the operation itself. Spotters had to watch the forest edge to check trespassers, small planes had to be diverted, troops and police had to be moved away, local Africans had to be warned, and farmers, forest scouts, game scouts and fish wardens had to be asked not to go near the forest fringe. When all this had been done, the planning of the operation could go forward.

By the night of the 7th of October, all preparations had been completed, the weather was still fine and we were ready to move. A long convoy of vehicles, all covered with tarpaulins to keep the terrorists hidden, pulled out of Mayfield and set course for the Aberdares, which we reached after dawn so that the lights of the vehicles would not be seen from the forest above.

This time two main base camps were set up, the first deep in the forest on the Kinaini river and the second high up on the edge of the Moorlands in an area called Karandi ka gitara-ini, which, as the name was something of a tongue-twister for the wireless operators, we renamed 'Frost Camp' after an early visit when Mac and I spent several minutes looking for a spare wheel which we had tossed out of the back of a Land Rover when we went to sleep and which had been completely hidden beneath a mattress of frost when we began to look for it the following morning.

Kinaini Camp was sited in the area where there were probably more hyrax than in any other part of the Aberdares. The noise they made at night was so great that we found it difficult to sleep, but it had the advantage of drowning the normal noise and clatter of camp life. We could not resist catching one of these lovely, softskinned but ferocious little creatures and it stayed with us as a mascot in a little pen beside the camp fire throughout the operation.

One of the snags about Kinaini Camp was the fact that it was surrounded by thickly forested hills which badly interfered with wireless transmission. This compelled us to erect a dipole several hundred yards away at the top of one of these hills and we had to climb up there every time there was a message to be passed. Doing this at night without torches was not a popular occupation.

When the camp was first set up, the river on which we depended for water was a muddy brown and the mixture of leaves, broken twigs and branches made the water almost undrinkable. During the rains that sort of thing was to be expected but in the dry season the culprits could only be elephant. Luckily the herds moved on elsewhere and our water supply improved before we became too desperate.

By the following evening, the 6th of October, most of the sorting out at the camp had been done and we were as comfortable as possible. At Kinaini Camp, the lower base, the accent was on protection against big game, particu-

larly rhino, who are a particular menace at night when
camp fires are burning. All bivouacs were erected beside trees which could be climbed easily. The fires were
sited so that they were ringed with vehicles. Petrol was
spilt on nearby paths used by big game coming down to
the river to drink. At Frost Camp the emphasis was on
keeping warm. All the bivouacs were pitched where the
ground was not too damp. Firewood was collected lower
down the mountain in the bamboo belt and stacked in
large bundles at the base, for as soon as the rains broke the
tracks would become impassable and no more could be
fetched. But of even greater importance than firewood
were the Hexamine cookers and their solid fuel tablets
which were stored in large quantities. The inventor of
these cookers was praised from the day we arrived at
Frost Camp until the day we left. When the firewood was
wet and it was pouring with rain, these cookers were
placed in the backs of Land Rovers where everyone
huddled in search of warmth.

From these two camps our force set out early on the
morning of the 9th of October. There was a team for each
of the nine prayer trees, one for each of the two letter
boxes, one for each of the food stores and four for searching the trapping area south of the Ruhotie valley. In
addition another five teams were used for odd tasks such
as ambushing known gang routes and watching various
springs where it was thought Kimathi might be drawing
water. One reserve party consisting of two smaller teams
was held back at the camps, rationed and armed and
ready to move off at a minute's notice.

This operation would make us or break us. We knew
that if we failed to account for Kimathi this time, he would
disappear for many months, probably for years, probably
for ever. Our span of life, operationally speaking, was
about two weeks. After that the region would be so full

of our tracks that Kimathi would undoubtedly abandon it for good, knowing that a major force had been thrust against him and knowing that his favourite haunts had also become our favourite haunts. Once he realized this, once he realized we knew his fourteen key points, he would certainly vanish. He might cross through the settled areas and go into the vast forests of Mount Kenya; he might move into the sparsely inhabited regions of the Uaso Nyiro or go further into the Northern Frontier District, which he knew well; he might travel further and cross into Tanganyika or Ethiopia. He might even commit suicide and leave us hunting him for months after his death. He had talked about all these things, as I knew only too well.

By the night of the 9th, all our teams had reached their destinations. Those at the letter boxes found from a study of the tracks that two terrorists had visited the trees three or four days before. They had left behind withering branches, a sign, we believed, that they had picked up letters which had been left for them. This meant that Mbaka's two companions, who had disappeared over the crest of the hill during the last operation, had now rejoined Kimathi. There was good news from one of the teams at the food stores. They arrived to find that the new store contained a few pounds of dried buck meat which suggested that the process of building up a reserve supply of food had begun and should continue. Those teams moving into the trapping area and to the prayer trees arrived without mishap but found nothing of special interest to tell us.

This time we did not intend to lie up close beside the key points. In the first place, it was obvious that Kimathi would not go to any of them, be they his stores, his prayer trees, his letter boxes or his traps, unless he had sent his men ahead to see that all was safe. As long as he had any followers, he would expose them before he exposed himself. This meant that little good would come of ambushing the key points and capturing anyone who came along. Our plan this time was to hide a short distance from the key points, which would be visited by two men every few hours to find out if anyone had been to them. If someone had, the team would be called up and the fresh tracks of the visitors would be followed until they led to Kimathi. In effect, we were going to rely on tracking.

Secondly, the time factor was important. Our men could lie in ambush points without moving for three or four days, but after that they would become restless, bored and less careful about hiding. This meant that if Kimathi's gangsters did not visit any of the key points until the fifth or seventh or tenth day, there was every likelihood of our teams being seen and our operation compromised. We could not afford to run that risk.

The days passed all too quickly without further developments and with each day my anxiety mounted. All the time the forest was being plastered more and more with our tracks. We began to wonder whether the teams looking for traps south of the Ruhotie valley had been seen as they combed the forests; we wondered whether other teams had been spotted at the time of the move in. Why and where was Kimathi lying low?

On the fourth day, the 13th of October, runners were sent out to contact all the teams except those searching for traps, with whom we could not get into touch. We asked if Kimathi could have seen them or their tracks, but in each case they said that this could not have been so. Nevertheless, every hour produced more tracks and more evidence of our presence in the forest. Before we had prayed for the rains to hold off, now we prayed that the rains would come to obliterate every mark that we had made and give us a fresh start.

The rain birds, with their perpetual, incessant whistle, were heard all over the forest but that was little consolation as they had been whistling for several days.

Each morning the European and African staff left the camps and visited rendezvous points deep in the forest where reports were sent by the teams, but day after day the results were negative. As a distraction, we set a number of partridge traps near our two base camps. When a bird was caught, the other camp would be raised on the wireless and proudly informed of the achievement. Once when Busani at Kinaini Camp was hauled out of bed to be told by Gethieya at Frost Camp that his score had gone up by one, Busani retorted: 'That's nothing. Here we have just caught twelve and given them Patchetts and sent them back into the forest to hunt for Kimathi!' A camp without Busani was really no camp at all. This huge, strapping Mkamba, over six feet tall and weighing almost fourteen stone, a native of the hot country of Machakos, always had a smile on his face. He did not, however, have any special liking for climbing the steep slopes of the Aberdares. We all sympathized with him for having so much weight to drag along, but we could never look back and watch him toiling up the hills without bursting into laughter and this invariably made him collapse on the ground laughing heartily too. Yet although he was no mountaineer, his physical strength was colossal. With his massive shoulders and arms he could lift the back of a Land Rover clear off the ground when we wanted to change a wheel, a feat which gained him the nickname 'kereni' or crane among the terrorists.

As always, we had our moments with game. One day we saw a huge bull elephant feeding by itself in a valley beside Kinaini Camp. Accompanied by one of our terrorists, Mac and I went down to have a look at it. We reached a spot from where we had an excellent view of

this colossal beast but that was by no means near enough
for our companion, who dared us to accompany him
closer. We unwisely accepted the challenge and on we
went. Within a few minutes we entered an extremely
thick belt of muondwe scrub where none of us could see
more than a yard or two ahead. Suddenly, we were
horrified to see the bull only a few feet in front of us,
facing in our direction with its trunk upraised. With a
grunt, the terrorist shot past us and went crashing
through the undergrowth. Mac and I followed suit. We
dashed out of the muondwe belt and up the side of the
valley, where we paused, breathless, to glance back. Much
to our relief and surprise, the elephant was still standing
exactly where we had left him. With arms, legs and
clothes all torn and scratched, we trudged back to camp.
For two nights I dreamt about elephants!

Bill Eastbrook had a worse experience. He met two
large buffaloes on a track where, on the one side, there
was a vertical drop of some thirty feet and, on the other, a
steep cliff. Unluckily, the animals decided against running down the track away from him. Instead they
thundered up towards him and he had the hair-raising
experience of standing there with nothing larger than a
revolver in his hand, as they bolted past him, one on
either side. If he had run he would almost certainly have
been killed. I think this was the narrowest shave any of
the staff personnel experienced during the operation, for
being sandwiched between two galloping buffaloes is an
experience never to be forgotten.

Soon after this, Mac was driving his Land Rover
along Wanderer's track towards Frost Camp, quite unaware of danger, when a charging rhino rammed
the back of his vehicle. He had heard a crash behind him
and felt the back of the vehicle jump up. On looking
round, he was shocked to see the rhino close on his tail.

Accelerating furiously, he dashed into the camp, where the terrorists claimed that the rhino would not have charged him if it had not seen his moustache and mistaken it for the horns of a buffalo!

And so the first few days passed. I carried my lucky Arab-silver bracelet, still tied to a handkerchief, from camp to camp and we all hoped it would bring us luck in the days to come.

Chapter Twenty

LUCKY BEEHIVE

Mageria nimo mahota
Where there's a will there's a way.

WE were beginning to wonder whether the fourteen key points really were going to provide us with a lead to Kimathi when, on the afternoon of the 15th of October, events took a sharp turn for the better. Round about midday, a single terrorist from Kimathi's gang came to the letter box between the Muringato and Itha rivers and put a letter in the old beehive. An hour later, the team covering this point, on one of their routine visits, saw his tracks beneath the tree and found the letter in the hive. It was in Kimathi's own handwriting and read: 'I am still where you left me and you must come back when the store is full.'

It was quite clear that some of Kimathi's gangsters were away collecting food for storage. It was also clear that if we could find any of them, they would know exactly where we could find him. At the time it also seemed reasonably sure that Kimathi was somewhere nearby. Having put the letter back in the hive, two men were left in ambush while the rest of the team set off to follow up the lone terrorist's tracks. They eventually arrived at Frost Camp many days later after travelling nearly forty miles through the forest on a false trail. Somehow they had lost the tracks of Kimathi's man and got on to the tracks of another individual. These things do happen even with the best trackers.

Other developments were soon reported. In the area south of the Ruhotie valley, one of the trap-searching teams found the tracks of two other terrorists. These zig-zagged about all over the place and even doubled back on their original course. Only terrorists in search of suitable places to lay game traps would keep changing direction like this, yet that explanation did not seem to fit this case. Why should they twice return to ground they had already inspected? By dusk the team had not solved this problem and on the following morning, the 16th of October, they split up into pairs to sweep through the forest.

Half a mile south of the Ruhotie river, there is a swamp thickly covered with water-plants and tall ithanji reeds. While two of our men were edging their way through it, they thought they heard a rifle being loaded—the sound of a bolt being snapped forward and closed. Thinking they had run into Kimathi, both our men immediately blazed away into the reeds with their weapons. They heard a splash and they saw the tall reeds shaking further over to their left. Cautiously they advanced. But a few steps further on they heard something bubbling in the water. They looked down and saw Gitahi, Kimathi's most trusted veteran, who had been shot in the back and was now lying half-submerged in the water. They dragged him out and questioned him. There had been three terrorists in the reeds, 7 Kar, Ngunyi and himself. They had left Kimathi, Wanjiru and Maragua three days before, many miles up the mountains near Mihuro in the very thick bamboo while they had come down to trap buck and store meat in the newly made food store.

Gitahi was immediately talkative, probably because he was half-drowned, and agreed to lead our men back to

Kimathi's hiding place. No effort was made to search for his two companions. They would probably make for the beehive letter box where two of our men were already waiting. If they did so, all would be well, for they would be caught there, but if they rushed straight back to Kimathi and reached him before we did, the position would be most serious. Gitahi knew every one of the fourteen key points upon which our operation was based, and Kimathi might easily see to it that none of his men visited any of them again when he heard of Gitahi's capture.

It was a race against time. Fortunately, our two terrorists were sufficiently intelligent to realize this, so half-carrying, half-dragging their wounded prisoner, they made off as fast as they could for Kinaini base camp, which they reached at five past four that afternoon. Only three hours were left before nightfall. A strong team was quickly prepared, a bush stretcher was made to carry Gitahi, the assault had to be planned and the siting of supporting teams had to be decided. While Gitahi's wound was being dressed, runners were sent hurrying off to contact all the teams by the letter boxes, the food stores and prayer trees to tell them to move in beside their key points and ambush them. Other runners were sent to recall those teams ambushing forest paths and water points well out of range of Kimathi's present position. A third group went off to recall the teams looking for game traps south of the Ruhotie valley.

At four o'clock there were only sixteen terrorists available at Frost Camp and Kinaini Camp. Once the assault team had been picked and the runners sent off, only three men were left.

The task allotted to the runners that crucial evening was particularly dangerous. Not only did they run a grave risk of being mistaken for hostile terrorists by the teams, whom they would reach long after dark, but they faced a tremendous threat from wild game. It was bad enough to go through the Tree Tops salient in the daytime, but to go through it at night, and alone, must have been hair-raising. However bad their background, however shady their characters, we raised our hats to these runners.

As far as it is humanly possible to know a forest well, we knew the area where Kimathi was said to be lurking. The bamboo there was so thick and interwoven that a noiseless approach was physically impossible. That was probably the reason he had chosen to stay there. It was a place where his enemies could not creep up on him with-out being heard. He would probably hear us a hundred yards away and run for it, but then he too would make a noise—a noise which we could follow. Only the fastest and most agile of our available men were chosen for the assault team.

We left only one man in Frost Camp and one in Kinaini Camp, all the others, including the sick, were mustered and armed. Within half an hour of Gitahi's arrival our transport was grinding up the mountain with accelera-tors hard down on the floorboards. At the 9,400-feet mark, the main assault team, led by the ever-faithful Gati, dropped off and disappeared into the forest with Gitahi bouncing up and down on a stretcher. A little further on, we sent off three two-man teams to ambush three fords that Kimathi might use. The time was exactly 6.16 p.m. when the last team took up its position. Twenty-six miles had been covered since the vehicles left Kinaini Camp, twenty-six miles up a rough, moun-tainous track in one hour and ten minutes.

That night was certainly one to remember. Laurie Pearse and Jim Stephen, lying in ambush at one of Kimathi's favourite track-crossing points, were almost trampled by a rhino which came up on them so quickly and silently in the darkness that they first saw its massive black form a few yards away. Gethieya and a terrorist, ambushing at another track-crossing, were put to flight by some large, aggressive beast which they could not identify. Opposite Ruhuru-ini hill, a team of two terrorists became entangled in a pack of African wild dogs. The dogs were running down a bushbuck which ran between our ambushers and brought the pack down on top of them. For several minutes there was a great deal of growling and snarling, but fortunately nothing worse happened. An otter bit the heel of one of the men on the Chania river ford and the single terrorist left on guard at Kinaini Camp, feeling somewhat hungry, ate a tin of Simonize car polish thinking it was butter.

Meanwhile our assault team had problems of its own. After leaving the vehicles, Gati's team had only carried Gitahi on the stretcher a short way before they found they could not get it through the tangled mass of bamboo, so they threw it away and lifted Gitahi on their shoulders. But Gitahi soon found that this was too uncomfortable and, despite his wound, decided to walk, which, incredibly, he did.

Just before darkness fell they got within one hundred and fifty yards of Kimathi's hide-out. There they halted while Gitahi stretched out his arm and pointed out its rough position to them. They could not see the hide-out itself but they could make out the clump of bamboo beside it quite easily and that was a good enough pinpoint. Leaving Gitahi behind, the team split up. After turning towards Mount Kenya and praying for a few seconds, they rushed the hide-out from three sides. But it was empty. The care with which Kimathi had covered up all his tracks, the care with which he had buried the ashes of the fire, the care with which he had ruffled the grass where he lay, was proof that he had not left in a hurry. He had moved house. The team called up Gitahi and all sat down in the hide-out to discuss their next move. Had Kimathi dreamt again? But one thing was certain, his departure had not been inspired by Ngunyi or 7 Kar, for then he would have leapt away without making such elaborate arrangements. In any case, the hide-out had been abandoned long before the action in the camp.

Huddled together round Gitahi, who was shivering from cold and shock, the team reviewed the facts. Soon they came to the conclusion that they had been rather stupid ever to suppose that Kimathi would be there. After all, he would not normally stay in a place known to men who were out of his sight for fear that they would be captured and guide the Security Forces back to him. That was a risk he would hate to take. The fact that he had said in his letter 'I am still where you left me' did not necessarily mean that he was still in the same hide-out. He would say this in any case to let his absent followers know that all was well.

In our team there were four terrorists who had once belonged to Kimathi's gang. They now recalled many previous occasions when Kimathi had left letters saying he was in a given place whereas, in fact, he had been *in the vicinity*. That was what he always meant—he was never to be taken too literally—and it would be up to his men to search for him. This time, they thought Kimathi was probably expecting Gitahi, 7 Kar and Ngunyi to look for him anywhere in the bamboo belt within two miles of the hide-out.

As there was little more than three-quarters of an hour of daylight left, it would normally have been preferable to spend the night quietly in the hide-out and begin a search of the surrounding forest early in the following morning, but this was not a normal occasion. Nobody could tell whether Ngunyi and 7 Kar were already searching for Kimathi. The hunt had to continue, even by night.

Leaving three men in the hide-out to deal with 7 Kar and Ngunyi, if they arrived, the rest of the team, with Gitahi, set off towards the only spring in the area, which was less than half a mile away. That was the place where the gang had watered before Gitahi went down the mountain, and as Kimathi would never drink at a river—the noise would prevent his hearing the approach of his enemies—it was the only place nearby from which he could draw water. Within a few minutes they were there and began to examine the ground. The sun had already fallen behind the mountain and the light was poor, but they were able to see that the spring was still in use. They could just see one set of tracks leading away up a slope and winding on through the bamboo. Gitahi was pushed into the lead and the hunt began.

They had not gone more than two hundred yards when Gitahi suddenly dropped to the ground. Like a row of skittles, everyone behind him fell down and lay still. Gitahi swung his left hand slowly round behind him and clawed at the soft earth with his fingers as a signal to Gati to creep up beside him. '*Kabuci Kau*,' ('There's the hide-out,') he whispered. Gati raised his head slightly and peered through the bamboo. There, about thirty yards in front of him, was a buckskin coat hanging on a branch and three cooking sticks jutting out of the ground below it. For several minutes the team lay completely quiet to see if they could hear anything moving about, but all was silent. Then they crept forward, some going round the side, others round the back, until they had surrounded the cooking sticks. Once again, the hide-out was empty. But this time there was a difference. Stuck away under a little bush was a heap of newly cut thabai or wild nettle and an old pot; beside this was a leg and the ribs of a buck; near the entrance were two skin bags and a tattered army blanket; further over, beside a bed of flattened grass, were two rusty bully-beef tins— Kimathi's cups. Looking around more carefully, Gati found two lengths of trapping wire rolled up neatly on sticks and placed at the foot of the 'bed'. And under the thabai was Kimathi's Kikuyu Bible, the only book he had not burnt. Here lay Kimathi's worldly wealth, with the sole exception of his revolver and the leopard-skin jacket which he wore, a jacket he had taken from his brother, Wambararia.

Our men spread out to wait for Kimathi's return. They were confident that at long last his day had come.

They waited while the elephant, the rhino, the wild dogs and the otter were terrorizing or aggravating our lonely ambushers. They waited while the moon rose high. They waited while the partridges began to call at dawn. Still there was no sign of Kimathi.

Far away down the mountain, all but one of the runners had by this time contacted their teams. From that moment, Kimathi's letter boxes, his food stores and his favourite prayer trees were closely ambushed. As the night of the 16th of October faded, we cut Kimathi's lifeline.

Chapter Twenty-one

HIS FINAL HOURS

Kuhonoka ti gutura

To pass through danger once is
no guarantee for the next time

or

To escape is not to survive.

WHEN Kimathi did not return to his hide-out by dawn
on the 17th of October, Gati's team split into two groups.
One half waited at the hide-out, the other began a search
of the surrounding forest. By now five other teams that
had arrived at Kinaini Camp shortly after day-break
were being rationed, briefed, and brought round through
the forest to close in on the Mihuro area.

Then, to our delight, a heavy shower of rain fell over
most of the eastern Aberdares. We knew that this would
obliterate all the tracks we had left in the forest during
the previous eight days. It would also make it very difficult for Kimathi to break away from Mihuro without
leaving tracks of his own.

Soon there was more good news. All three of the buck
traps laid by Gitahi, 7 Kar and Ngunyi many days before
were found and removed by our men. We knew that
when this phase of operations against Kimathi began,
his gang had seven trapping wires. The removal of these
three in the Ruhotie and the discovery of the two in his
hide-out left him with two. If these were found, he would
be unable to trap and this would force him to seek food

in the Kikuyu reserve. This, in turn, would expose him to the Kikuyu Guard, the regular Security Forces and all the other dangers that beset a terrorist who leaves the forest. His only alternative would be to visit the new food store under the large fig tree in the Ruhotie valley, but there we were already waiting for him.

The rain had barely stopped, the forest was still dripping, when a team led by Ruku was shot at. They did not see their enemy, but they had no doubt who it was. Spreading out quickly, they raced forward, but after running two hundred yards, Ruku trod on a stump and badly injured his foot. He fell while his men ran on out of sight. He was left alone, far behind, bandaging his foot with a strip of dirty cloth. As he was sitting there, he realized that he was not alone. Rising to his feet, his bandage still only half tied, he looked around. At that precise moment, he saw Kimathi walk out of a thick clump of bamboo and start across a small clearing about thirty feet away. Kimathi's long black plaited hair was hanging down over his face and shoulders. His arms were hidden beneath his large leopard-skin coat and he was wet through from the rain. For a moment Ruku could not believe his eyes. Then, he nervously lifted his Patchett automatic, aimed at Kimathi's moving body and squeezed the trigger. There was a loud click as the bolt sprang forward, but the weapon did not fire. Kimathi turned round, looked straight at Ruku, and instantly put his hands in front of his face as though to shield his eyes from a burst of bullets. Ruku grabbed the bolt of his gun and drew it back to reload, but Kimathi was already turning away and running for cover with his hands now crossed behind his head. Ruku aimed again and pulled the trigger, but still the weapon did not fire. Seconds later, Kimathi had disappeared.

With a heavy heart, Ruku limped away to rejoin his

DEDAN KIMATHI
DURING HIS TRIAL AT NYERI

R. V. Gillman

men. Dumbfounded, they listened as he told them his story. They stripped his weapon to find out why it had failed to fire, but they could find nothing wrong with it. They went back to the clearing where they examined Kimathi's tracks. They saw where Ruku had stood and where Kimathi had dashed out of sight. After the rain his trail was clear, and they followed it.

We had never disputed the fact that Kimathi was abnormally lucky, but this was the last straw. After many months of toil and hardship, we had finally got him within our grasp, staring into the muzzle of a loaded sub-machine gun, and yet he had escaped unscathed. The effect of this mishap on the rest of the terrorists in our force was easy to foresee. They would have been convinced that he was immortal. Some would have regarded the incident as a sign of Ngai wanting him to remain alive. Fortunately, very fortunately, events followed this one in such quick succession that no one had time to brood.

The first of Kimathi's two remaining traps was found by Gati's team within a hundred yards of the spring at ten o'clock that morning. By two o'clock in the afternoon, we had located the second trap. As some of Gati's men approached it, they heard Kimathi's high-pitched voice call out, 'Who is there?' He was standing about forty yards to one side of the trap hidden in the forest. One of our men shouted back, 'It is us.' 'Who?' shouted Kimathi abruptly. '7 Kar,' said our man, but Kimathi would have none of it and as he took to his heels he shouted to Wanjiru, 'Mother of the Gods, be caught by yourself!'

With Gati's team chasing them, Kimathi, Maragua (Kimathi's last male companion) and Wanjiru ran through the forest. Then there was firing ahead. They had bumped into Gacheru's team coming up from the Zaina

I

valley. Gacheru shot at Maragua. Gacheru saw him fall
as though wounded, then rise and run on, carrying a rifle.
Gitero fired a long burst at some shaking leaves, but it
was one of Gacheru's men. Everything was happening
quickly. Friend and foe were jumbled together firing
indiscriminately at everything that moved. Then Kimathi was seen again. He was standing behind a bush as
one of our men named Mugo ran out. Kimathi shot
with his revolver at point-blank range, but missed. Mugo
shot back, but Kimathi had already slipped behind a
tree and was off through the undergrowth. Ruku's team,
who had been following Kimathi's tracks and getting
closer and closer to him, heard the running gun battle
and raced up to join in the mêlée. Within minutes they
too saw Kimathi for a split second, shot at him, missed
and then chased after him. From time to time Kimathi
and Maragua fired back at their pursuers. Nderitu,
from Gati's team, armed only with a simi, caught up with
Kimathi, and was about to slash him down from behind
when Kimathi turned and fired at him. The bullet passed
through Nderitu's skin coat, grazing his stomach. He fell
back, too shocked to go on.

Then Maragua broke away from Kimathi and was
seen climbing a steep cliff towards the Moorlands, dragging his rifle along the ground by its muzzle. Bullets
kicked up the earth round him, but he reached the top
and disappeared over the brow. A few yards further on,
Wanjiru fell exhausted, and was captured. She swore at
her captors, spat at them, bit them and kicked at them
as they bound her up. Most of our men were also tiring
after the hot pace, and crowded round her, but a few
raced on after stopping momentarily to look at the
woman who had out-run and out-fought them before.
Now Kimathi was alone! He had seen his woman fall
but he never paused to help her. He had seen Maragua

break away with his only remaining rifle. He knew he could never find 7 Kar or Ngunyi again. Perhaps they had led his hunters on to him and he did not want to see them again anyway. Like a frightened buck, gifted with that extra strength which only the fringe of death can provide, he fled on through the forest. The chase continued for another two miles. Now and then our men heard Kimathi ahead but he was gaining on them. For the last time he vanished into the forest.

That evening, Wanjiru, wearing a dirty buckskin garment and still bleeding from bad cuts on her legs, was brought to Kinaini Camp. She was lean, but wiry and very strong. For a Kikuyu girl, she had unusually sharp features and was not unattractive—she had after all been chosen by her master from all the hundreds of Kikuyu girls who went into the forest at the beginning of the emergency. There were scars all over her body which bore witness to the terrible life she had led in the jungle. We began to question her about her master's movements.

It turned out that Kimathi had not been alone when Ruku saw him in the glade. Wanjiru and Maragua had been waiting for him under a tree only a short distance away. After his miraculous escape, he had come running up to them and told them what had happened. All three had then headed west to collect their belongings from their hide-out before moving on to some other faraway area.

'Why didn't you go back to the hide-out last night?' asked Gati. 'Kimathi refused,' answered Wanjiru, who now told how the three of them had left the hide-out to check their two game traps. For some unexplained reason, Kimathi had decided to lie out in the forest for the night. Both she and Maragua had pleaded with him to return because they were hungry and there was buck meat and wild nettle there to be eaten, but he was reso-

lute in his refusal. When the rain started the following
morning, they had stood beneath a tree for shelter, and
when the storm passed Kimathi told them to wait until
he returned. Why he went, or where he went to nobody
knew, but it was during this lone journey that he had run
into Ruku.

All that night at Kinaini Camp we tried to decide
what Kimathi would do now that he was alone. We
thought he might go back to his hide-out to collect the
food and some of his possessions. The hide-out was already
ambushed. He might go to his food store in the Ruhotie
valley. We were already waiting for him there. He might
go to his letter boxes to look for Gitahi, Ngunyi and 7 Kar.
We were there too. He might go to a prayer tree. We
were watching every one that he was likely to visit. He
would be hungry and knowing that his last two traps in
Mihuro had been found, he might go to the Ruhotie
area to look for Ngunyi's three traps. We had already
removed them and there were teams in the area. He
could not boil wild nettle because his only cooking pot
was in his hide-out. He could not trap meat because he
had no traps. He could not live on honey because there
was none in the area. Unless he tried to find food in the
places where we were already waiting for him, he would
be forced to take the biggest risk of all—to go alone to
steal food in the populated Kikuyu reserve. But that was
the only course for which, apart from suicide, we had,
as yet, no solution. This was the only point on which we
needed Wanjiru's advice. At what point along the forest
edge would Kimathi enter the Kikuyu reserve when
hunger forced his hand? Wanjiru knew her Kimathi well
and we knew he would confide in her far more than he
would in any of his men. He had probably already discussed with her the route they would take to enter the
reserve, if the worst were to happen; but even if he had not

done so, her opinion would be worth a great deal, for she knew which areas Kimathi thought were safe and which he thought were dangerous.

Three female terrorists in our force were first put with Wanjiru in the hope that she would give them information that she would not give to the men, but despite many hours of talk, she would not co-operate with them. 'There is nothing,' she repeated, 'which would make Kimathi go near the reserve.' Then some of our men took her aside and tried to talk her round, but all she would say to them was, 'How could I know which route you would take if you were chased from here?' I then tried myself, but it was no good. She refused to look at me. As she spoke she gazed at the ground. She refused to eat or drink anything because, as she said, 'You might have bewitched it.' As a last resort, Gitahi and some of Kimathi's old guard were sent off to talk to her in a quiet, secluded place. They chatted for hours and hours in a circle round a little fire, then when the dawn's winds rose, they moved to a small bivouac where, huddled together, they continued the conversation. By daybreak her old comrades had won her over. She named two possible places on the forest edge where Kimathi was most likely to cross into the native reserve. Instead of being stubbornly loyal to her master as she had been the evening before, she now grew angry whenever anyone referred to her as 'Kimathi's woman' and instead of refusing food, she drank some gruel and ate several pounds of meat. She had suddenly come to hate Kimathi. This was a typical example of the Mau Mau mentality. For hours, or even weeks, a hardened supporter of Mau Mau will lean one way with utmost stubbornness, resisting every argument and every new idea, then, suddenly, some minute factor produces a fantastic change and the victim leans the other way, often with equal stubbornness. Normally, that vital, minute chink in their mental armour can only be found by persons whose minds work in the same way.

The two places on the forest edge where Kimathi would cross were, according to Wanjiru, a point opposite the Kikuyu village of Kihuyo in Tetu Location, or a point near the Zaina river. As we could not risk putting our own terrorists at either of these places for fear that they would be shot at either by the Security Forces or the Kikuyu Guard, we had no alternative to calling up conventional forces to cordon the forest edge at those two vital points. We sent an urgent signal to Nyeri, early on the morning of the 18th of October, asking for help, and within two hours, Colonel Eric Hayes-Newington, Operational Staff Officer at Provincial Police Headquarters in Nyeri, arrived at Kinaini base camp. He brought with him a letter of encouragement from the Commander-in-Chief, Lieut.-General Sir Gerald Lathbury.

Some other teams were now reporting to Frost Camp. They were quickly rationed and moved down the mountain, but they were warned not to work as low down as the forest edge where Colonel Eric had been asked to establish a string of night-time ambushes.

Then for the first time we had a spare moment to examine Ruku's Patchett. The wrong type of 9 mm. ammunition had been issued to Ruku and this had caused the jam when Kimathi walked in front of him.

That night, units of the King's African Rifles and Kenya Police took up ambush positions on the forest edge opposite Kihuyo village, while units of tribal police and tribal police reserve formed a stop line along the forest edge between Njogu-ini and the Zaina river. The eastern flank was secure.

Kimathi's movements after his escape from the fight

at Mihuro show very clearly that he, too, knew that his end was near. From one o'clock on the 17th of October, when he was last heard disappearing through the bamboo, until four o'clock the following afternoon, he did not rest once, not even long enough to drink. First he headed north towards the National Park track, then he swung sharply to the west and climbed up the slopes, then he turned south and raced on until he reached Chania hill, then he went east again, down the mountain slopes, as though he was making for the Kikuyu reserve. When he was about eight miles from the reserve he went north again, thus completing a full circle. He did not cross the National Park track at any of his usual crossing places, nor did he choose a spot where the forest was thick and safe, but dashed across an open space where no terrorist would normally tread. Then back in the Tree Tops salient, he stumbled on for several miles, still going north, until he reached the steep valley of the Mwathe. Finally, at about four o'clock on the afternoon of the 18th of October, after travelling non-stop for just under twenty-eight hours and covering a distance of almost eighty miles, he collapsed within half a mile of the forest edge at Njogu-ini. There he spent the night lying out in the ghostly forest, as he had done more than a thousand times before, but this time he was absolutely alone.

After dawn on the 19th of October, Kimathi made no effort to leave the forest edge. He crept along the fringe, eyeing the Kikuyu working in the Tetu Location, until he reached a point where he could look down on Karuna-ini, the place where he had spent much of his youth. There he sat gazing across the hilly country dotted with wattle trees and banana plantations, and there he drank some water from a stream. All day he sat, but as night fell, hunger drove him on. Before the moon rose, he crossed the deep ditch on the forest edge which had been dug earlier in the emergency to stop food carriers taking supplies to the gangs in the forest, and for the first time in more than forty months, he set foot in the Kikuyu reserve. He stripped some sugar cane and a few unripe bananas from a nearby plot and darted back to the forest to eat them. Our ambush parties should have spotted him but his luck had not quite deserted him.

By the morning of the 20th of October, several of our teams were moving on the forest edge, as by this time we had found the place where Kimathi had collapsed near Njogu-ini and it was clear that he was somewhere along the edge. Twice during the day Mac and I left the forest and circled round through the reserve to various points along the ditch to try to see that none of our teams reached the fringe and clashed with the army, police and tribal police ambush parties.

Events were now largely out of our hands. The machine could grind on without direction and late on the morning of the 20th of October I left the Aberdares and flew down to Nairobi. That afternoon my wife and I were presented to Her Royal Highness Princess Margaret at a garden party at Government House. It was, as the Americans would say, quite a contrast.

I had planned to spend forty-eight hours in Nairobi and return to the forest at dawn on the 22nd of October, but Kimathi's luck did not hold out long enough for that. After wandering silently along the forest edge on the 20th, he again crossed the ditch that night. Again he passed our guards, who did not see him in the darkness, and again he stripped some foodstuffs from a small plot, this time deeper in the reserve. But at 6.30 a.m. on Sunday the 21st, as he was sneaking back to the forest with the food he had stolen, he was seen by a party of six Kikuyu tribal policemen just as he was recrossing the ditch. While trying to climb out of the ditch into the forest, he was challenged by a tribal policeman called Ndirangu Mau. Kimathi ran down the ditch, Ndirangu fired three shots at him. Two missed. The third knocked him down. He got up again, climbed out of the ditch and rolled into the forest. Kimathi could not get far and almost immediately he was found, still wearing his leopard-skin coat, lying under a bush a few yards inside the forest. He had been severely wounded in the thigh. His revolver was found strapped to his body under his skin jacket.

The three shots were clearly heard by our teams near the forest edge. They knew it could only mean that Kimathi had been seen. They quickly spread out in the undergrowth, parallel to the forest edge in case he had escaped and was running towards them. But Kimathi did not appear. He was taken first to Ihururu, the chief's centre, from which he had escaped right at the beginning of the emergency. From there he was removed to hospital in Nyeri.

A strong cordon of police was thrown round the Nyeri hospital, not to prevent Kimathi's escape, but to stop crowds of angry Kikuyu, whose sons and daughters and mother and fathers had been murdered by his fanatical followers, from dragging him out and tearing him limb from limb.

Kimathi was operated on that afternoon and later removed to the Nyeri prison hospital, where a platoon of the Police General Service Unit mounted guard over him. As the days passed his condition improved steadily and within three weeks he was passed medically fit to stand his trial.

The case was heard by the Supreme Court of Kenya sitting at Nyeri. Every day the courtroom was crowded with curious spectators who were anxious to see what Kimathi looked like. As each witness filed into the witness-box, Kimathi stared at him in the same way as he had once stared at his victims and enemies in the forest.

After many days of argument the Judge summed up the evidence. Then the three African assessors gave their opinions. They all found that Kimathi was guilty. Finally the Judge pronounced the verdict and sentenced Kimathi to be hanged. The prisoner showed no emotion. It had been a fair and thorough trial by any standard. It was quite a contrast with his 'trials' in the forest.

Kimathi was then removed from Nyeri prison and taken under strong escort to the main Nairobi gaol. There he remained while his appeal was argued and dismissed. There, four and a half months later, he was executed.

And so the hunt for Dedan Kimathi ended. He was hardly a political figure, but he was a criminal of the first rank. It was appropriate that he should fall at last to a party of Kikuyu tribal policemen, representatives of that gallant body of tribal loyalists who had stood firm with Government and decency when the star of Mau Mau seemed to be rising. It was a final illustration of the great part that the Kikuyu people themselves played in the defeat of Mau Mau. The young Kikuyu children of the future would be able to stand outside their homes and look up at the distant mountain and say: 'That is where an evil past is buried.'

After visiting Kimathi in the hospital at Nyeri, I went straight back into the forest to unwind our operation and stand down the oddest army that ever fought for Queen and country in the history of the British Empire. Runners were sent out to bring all our teams back to Kinaini Camp. During the next forty-eight hours they trickled into camp tired out and weary. Gati was almost the last to arrive, lagging far behind the rest of his men, walking slowly, picking at his teeth with a piece of stick. He was deep in thought.

When I saw him coming, I went over and took him aside. We sat beneath the shade of a big tree to talk. 'Well, it's all finished, Gati,' I said. 'Yes, Kinyanjui,' he replied, 'it finished as Kingori prophesied—in the tenth month before the rains for millet planting began.' Then I remembered Kingori's words in prison some six months before. The prophecy had been fulfilled.

The last ambush team from the prayer trees was now coming into our camp. Of all Kimathi's prayer trees, those mugumo trees to which he had made his pilgrimages in search of his god Ngai, there was one which had attracted him more than the rest. Perhaps its shape or its surroundings fitted more accurately with the mugumo tree he had seen in his dream when 'god had taken him by the right hand and led him to it'.

This tree stood in the part of the forest which the Mau Mau called Kahiga-ini. It was an enormous tree with a huge trunk and heavy, hanging branches which reached almost to the ground. It had stood there for many years, probably since the turn of the century. Now our team came over to make their last report—the mugumo tree had fallen.

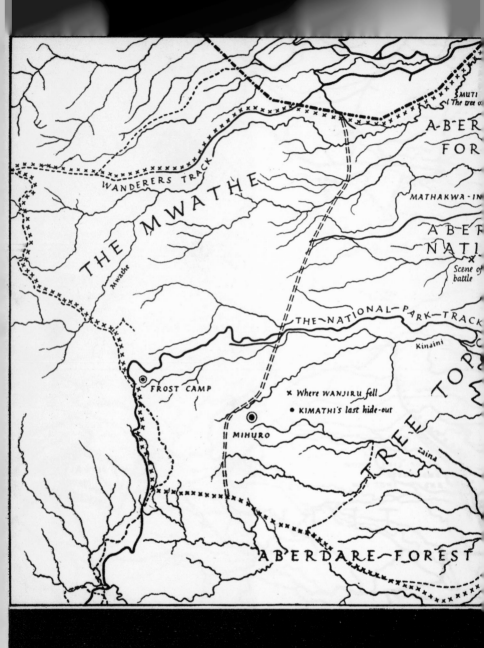

The Aberdare area where the operations
against Dedan Kimathi were carried out